Business Ethics
Theory

By

John Thanopoulos, Professor, University of Piraeus

Panagiotis Petratos, Professor, California State University, Stanislaus

2016

About the Authors

Dr. John Thanopoulos started his career as a business practitioner having achieved by the age of 26 more than $25,000,000 in sales. Eventually, however, he joined the academe and, from 1992, he became a professor of Marketing and International Business at the University of Akron in Ohio where he received various awards, among them for "Teaching Excellence" (1988), "Distinguished Sales and Marketing" (1994), "Publication" (1997) and "Teaching Innovation" (1997). Moreover, he was named by the Editors of Global Survey of the Academy of International Business as one of the six pioneers of these studies (2000) and by the World Education Congress as the "Best Professor in International Business" (2012). He also served to various other positions, including Academic Dean for the American College of Greece and Co-chair of the Executive Committee of the Greater Akron Export Association.

His academic contributions appeared in a variety of media, including editorships, texts, chapters in books, proceedings, case studies and journal articles like *Journal of Economic Integration, Review of Business, Journal of Teaching in International Business, Journal of International Business Studies, The International Trade Journal, Issues in International Business, Kyukyo Economic Review, Arkansas Business and Economic Review, Journal of the Academy of Marketing Science, Health Marketing Quarterly, Current Research in Global Business*, etc. In 2000 he returned to his homeland, Greece, joining the University of Piraeus at the Department of Business Administration as a professor of international business and since 2010 the graduate program of the Schools of Philosophy of the University of Athens and the University of Peloponnese teaching workplace ethics. In September 2015 he joined IST as a Professor and Dean of Business and Economics. His most recent books in Greek (all published by Interbooks or by Phedimos, Athens, Greece) are in international business (2002, 2006, 2012, and 2013; also, in 2007, in English), in ship management (co-authored, 2005) in business ethics (2003, 2009 and 2013) and in self-actualization perspectives of the international manager (co-authored, electronic format, 2010). His latest English book, *Global Business and Corporate Governances,* was published in 2014 by BEP, New York.

This lesson,
Post mortem and after many years of silence,
I owe it and dedicate it, to my Parents

Dr. Panagiotis Petratos PhD (Bedfordshire) MSEE (Wichita) MLE (Harvard) is alumnus Harvard University Management and Leadership in Education Graduate School of Education. Research and teaching experience includes Bell Laboratories, Intel Corporation, National Institute for Aviation Research USA, University of California Merced, California State University Stanislaus, University of Piraeus and Athens Institute for Education and Research. He is also elected Fellow Institution of Engineering and Technology (FIET), British Computer Society (FBCS), Institute of Mathematics and its Applications (FIMA), Higher Education Academy (FHEA), registered Chartered Engineer (CEng), European Engineer (EurIng), International Professional Engineer (IntPE), life member ΒΑΨ, ΒΓΣ, IEEE-HKN, senior member IEEE. Dr. Petratos also assists philanthropic causes for underprivileged people of Israel, Greece as well as humanitarian and environmental causes. Publications include numerous co-edited books, book chapters, as well as articles in peer reviewed International Conference Proceedings and Journals including *Journal of Emerging Markets, Review of Business Research, International Journal of Sustainability in Higher Education, Journal of Communication and Computer, Journal of Issues in Informing Science and Information Technology, Interdisciplinary Journal of Information, Knowledge and Management.*

To George
Deeply indebted dedicated to my father.
For my father everything is possible.

Business Ethics Theory

John Thanopoulos[1] Professor, University of Piraeus
Panagiotis Petratos[1] Professor, California State University, Stanislaus

Summary Table of Contents

Introduction: Dear co-citizen of the planet Earth
Chapter 1: From philosophy to ethics
Chapter 2: The society of the 21st century
Chapter 3: The era of the global corporation
Chapter 4: The market and customer
Chapter 5: The center of our attention: The employees!
Chapter 6: The environment, our home
Chapter 7: Finance issues and the code of corporate conduct
Epilogue: Living together

Table of Contents

Introduction: Dear co-citizen of the planet Earth

The ethics of international business

"Ethos: In Greek ἦθος character, a person's nature or disposition", is the etymology listed in Oxford English Dictionary and in reference to ancient aesthetic criticism and rhetoric: "Aristotle's statement that Polygnotus excelled all other painters in the representation of 'ethos' meant simply that his pictures expressed 'character'; but as Aristotle elsewhere says that this painter portrayed men as nobler than they really are, some modern writers have taken ethos to mean 'ideal excellence'."[2,3]

Robins also observes that "The intellectual life of Europe as a whole -the philosophical, ethical, political and aesthetic thought- draws its origin from the work of Greek philosophers and even today, we are all revisiting what remains from the intellectual activity of the Greeks, seeking stimulation and encouragement." [4]

Ethics according to Oxford English Dictionary is the branch of philosophy that deals with evaluative judgments on the distinction of good from evil and seeks to clarify the purpose of human life, and the means to achieve this worthy aim to live enareta, with virtue.

Reflecting on the Ethics definition one may deduce that Business Ethics is the evaluative judgment of business conduct distinguishing good from evil, seeking to clarify the purpose of business and the means to achieve this worthy aim with virtue and business ethos for the benefit of employees, customers, owners, consumers, our fellow humans, the society and the environment.

---

[2] "ethos, n.". OED Online. December 2012. Oxford University Press. 24 February 2013. <http://www.oed.com/view/Entry/64840?redirectedFrom=ethos&>.
[3] 1875 A. S. Murray in Encycl. Brit. II. 359 By ethos, as applied to the paintings of Polygnotus, we understand a dignified bearing in his figures, and a measured movement throughout his compositions, see also *Poetics* 1450ª28, *Poetics* 1448ª5.
[4] Robins R H, A short History of Linguistics, London Longman 1990.

In the mid-18th century Jeremy Bentham studied the utilitarian branch of philosophy and was one of the founders of the Classical School with the argument that crime, deviance and unethical conduct, were products of the exercise of free will. Bentham is considered by many the father of modern criminology[5].

Reflecting on Bentham's epicheirema one may deduce that human nature with tendencies of deviance is egoistical, narcissistic, hedonistic, aplestos, greedy, self-serving always preferring to take the easy path instead of the virtuous, honest, hard-working and painful path to achievement. This negatively portrayed deviant human nature is the complete opposite of ethos and ethical behavior which are only cultivated by positive characteristics of human nature such as altruistic, philanthropic, epicuric and assistive to avail good utility to our fellow humans. From teleological point of view ethical objectives are valuable aims worth pursuing. Ethical aims will benefit ourselves and based on the principle of reciprocity the products and services of our ethical work will be useful to our fellow humans.

Perhaps you have heard the story of the oil tanker ship which was deliberately neglected by its owner who insured it for a significant sum and operated it without required periodic maintenance and repairs causing it to sink, to create an environmental catastrophe and to carry with it tens of sailors to their death.

It is not unlikely that you have also heard the story of the hazardous materials plant that was operated by its owner with great economy and without the necessary safety measures causing a massive explosion and the death of hundreds of employees.

Probably you have also heard the story of the company which filed for bankruptcy in the USA leaving thousands of customers without the products they had already paid and relocating business operations in another offshore locale beyond the reach of the law to continue business as usual.

---

[5] Bentham, Jeremy. An Introduction to the Principles of Morals and Legislation (Collected Works of Jeremy Bentham). Clarendon Press, 1996.

How about the high tech corporation that outsourced manufacturing of all its products to an Asian supplier where working and living conditions led employees to suicide by jumping from high buildings? In order to address the issue safety nets were installed to catch future jumpers.

What about the argument of a politician stating "what is legal is also ethical…"? Reflecting on the speculation "what is legal is also ethical" a critical thinker may deduce that the reduction of ethics down to bare legality provides only the minimum of morality. In other words unscrupulous individuals who take advantage and exploit gaps and limitations of modern law can inflict significant financial or physical damage to law abiding citizens who seek and wish to follow ethical guidance in life by assisting themselves and their fellow humans. Hence, although the law can be fully enforced ethical pursuits cannot be involuntarily enforced on free will individuals.

The key question is: Do laws provide protection for law abiding citizens and prosecution, justice and punishment for business wrong doings? The answer is yes in most countries at least in theory and always given cultural constraints. In theory if the wrong doer is caught in the act of breaking the law and if there is political will, the wrong doer is punished in most cases.

However, the devil lurks in the details. Contemporary code of law has come a long way to address limitations and cover breaches created by socio-economical new order, scientific progress and business technological advances. Nonetheless law remains largely ambiguous, with a plethora of chasms, lacking necessary specialism for every field and every aspect of business. Such criticisms are not new and since 1809 Bentham has criticized the law of being an abyss of ambiguity to avail judges a convenient interpretation to use law in the interests of the government. [6]

Currently many of the western world well-developed governments are run by high-ranking managers-civil servants who often have a classical

[6] A Catechism of Parliamentary Reform." *Encyclopaedia Britannica* Inc., 2013. Web. 26 Feb. 2013. <http://www.britannica.com/EBchecked/topic/99338/A-Catechism-of-Parliamentary-Reform>

education and hold positions somehow relevant to their specialization. Often cutting-edge knowledge of their field is not critical to their advancement. Governments come and go however senior managers-civil servants remain. Instead of experienced medical doctors and nurses managing hospitals and the ministry of health, bureaucrats manage them. Instead of experienced educators managing the ministry of education, bureaucrats manage it. Hence the ambiguity and inefficiency of the government organization itself is perpetuated. If such is the state of affairs in the western world governments imagine how difficult, ambiguous and inefficient the state of government affairs is in the lesser-developed world. Therefore, in order to resolve these government management problems, we must allow for experienced professionals in their field to exercise management of their sectors. Sound and constantly upgraded specialization is a key factor to ethical management.

In addition if the law in a country of the western world is largely ambiguous with chasms and limitations which provide opportunity for unscrupulous individuals to take advantage and exploit them, imagine what the state of the law is in other parts of the world internationally.

In reality business owners know that international law has many limitations and for the most part of the world the laws of one country do not really apply to another country. There is also sufficient lack of international laws which allows individuals to find refuge in various countries with very accommodating laws and helpful legal authorities. All a business owner with criminal intent has to do in order to break the law without any consequences is to set up business operations in an international locale where the regional law allows wrong doing and the region lies outside the country borders of the legal jurisdiction she is trying to escape.

A tax paradise is a classic example of this where a country will impose no taxation to a business owner who relocates her business headquarters to one of these tax heavens or allow anonymous bank accounts without any imposed taxation.

Unfortunately there are no written laws on what is ethical and what is not, even if wrong doing becomes the cause for the poverty and demise of millions of people. There are no written laws regarding unethical theft or fraud or other unwritten criminal activities so that if the wrong doer is caught to pay for her unethical act.

As social beings we have learned virtues and ethics from our home, fellow humans, culture, and education. We have principles, ethics, and a code of social behavior. Laws are written for cases of violators who obviously break them. Laws are also meant to defend allowed behavior that society has accepted, in a specific country during a specified time period. In addition, the law usually provides boundaries that can be identified and measured and which have clear potential to control similar possible violations within the letter of the law.

Therefore, if we separate the two concepts, we can make the problem more obvious. The first concept is the *spirit* of the law which is meant to prevent all clear violators as well as unethical wrong doers which is the ideal. The second concept is the pragmatic legal writing and realistic application of the law which is limited in scope and boundaries.

Beyond the letter of the law begins the space of ethics. For example, we give the best quality uniforms to employees in our company, much more expensive than that required by law, because our business sees the initiative of protecting the well-being of our people as ethically correct. We offer to our customers the opportunity to return our products at any time because we consider it necessary according to our values to show respect to our customers. We strive to make a beautiful, clean and decent working environment because we want the same image for our business. We want society to believe that our business is ethical, principled, moral, and good. We want to adopt a business culture that attracts a particular type of employee, customer, and supplier. We want to establish corporate governance that has certain characteristics that vary according to our segment and the image of our company. For example, we will outline in a different way the corporate culture of a children amusement park and differently the culture of a business operator of casinos[7].

Naturally, the law is not the same in every country in the world and often legal loopholes are allowed, especially in less developed countries, where the local governments often lack the technology and scrutiny mechanisms required to enforce the law. To make this point in the human resource area, allow us to use the International Labor Rights Forum which publishes numerous reports on companies that use a range of tactics to violate the workers' right to organize in the workplace[8]. Are those reports violations of international business ethics?

There is an old euphemism that business organizations have no problem with ethics because they have none. Does "business" and "ethics" in the same sentence sound as oxymoron? Do we truly practice business ethics in business? Always? Better, if we can profit more without getting caught, aren't we willing to relax our ethical codes irrespective of the size of our company? Of course, the larger the size of our company, the more publicity we shall get for cases of wrong doing. For example, there were many criticisms in the business ethics and conduct of large corporations such as Enron, Global Crossing, Xerox, WorldCom, or Parmalat. Actions of questionable ethics and accounting irregularities led to law suits, investigations, damages, thousands of workers layoffs and many more catastrophes.

It is difficult to believe that corporations of such stature had not formulated solid ethical codes of business conduct and had no sense of corporate social responsibility. Responsibility, of course, is shared as well by the consulting companies and the auditors involved. Again in the case

---

[7] Probably one of first high-impact attempts from the professional press to establish awareness of the business ethics issue was Max Weber's, Business faces growing pressures to behave better, *Fortune*, May 1974, pages 193-195, 310, 314, 316, 319-320.
[8] Forget for the time being the word ethical! World-wide the human enterprise aims to save money since this is considered to be good business practice. For example see the ILRF report, "Working for Scrooge: Worst Companies of 2009 for the Right to Associate". At their site, www.ilrf.org, accessed August 16, 2012, you may find literary dozens of high-impact cases to read about. However, please use prudency, objectivity and culture-specific sensitivity when you are reading about similar cases. We shall return on the issues later in the text.

of Enron, McKinsey, one of the leading consulting companies with clients some of the largest corporations in the world, recommended Enron to follow a strategy of expansion called light-asset strategy, and perhaps this contributed to the spectacular bankruptcy of one of the largest US corporations[9]. Therefore, do business leaders investigate in advance the quality of their future advisors and auditors? Can business leaders do so without being influenced by existing networks or political pressures? Do business leaders manage to get the best consultants for their needs?

In the final analysis the reader may wonder if corporate misbehaving was built on strategic initiatives, the laws of the market, but also the socio-political laws, that have existed prior to the public outcry and the appalling human cost of unethical business actions. In the course of these events unethical managers and business leaders were revealed. Unfortunately, in society, sometimes we have people who violate the ethical laws because they have no conscience; often in these cases once they are discovered, it is too late.

Perhaps now is the right time to develop our effective awareness of ethical business choices and to put them in action in the overall business process. The business organization wherever located and regardless of size or industry, has now become a crucial part of society and must reflect the philosophy and ethics of the people.

Perhaps we are ahead of our time? Hundreds of millionaires with money inherited by family or wealth acquired by business activities seek to do good deeds for the people who are sick, unprivileged, underdeveloped, disadvantaged for humanitarian and environmental causes. Perhaps as some critics would say, in retrospect, they are more giving for reasons of social or posthumous fame.

The Gates and Buffets of the world, to mention only major international names, have the power and willingness to contribute to a better world,

---

[9] Source: John A. Byrne, Inside McKinsey, *BusinessWeek*, July 8, 2002 pages 54-62.

while others give awards and millions of dollars to African leaders to help them be just, rule without the temptation and without the lure of wealth[10].

In principle, such charitable actions are admirable. What is to become of thousands of people in dire poverty without the resources of the wealthy? However, none is to be questioned of where, how and what it took to generate all this money? Is there a parallel with the humanitarian considerations of some Kings who, with the money of government budgets, «endowed» poor girls? Was it their own money, and if not, how it was decided to provide, for example, to poor unmarried girls and not to minor orphans? History repeats itself so is currently a time like in the past when we were witnesses to a social tolerance that allows the very few and powerful to decide on the fates of many? When rich become even richer by betting on the desperation of the poor and selling them lotteries of happiness? Is it ethical to finance and support an educational system which rewards the people who follow instructions instead of personal inquiry? Is it ethical for mass media to advertise a material paradise and at the same time to develop habitual social behaviors of a passive nature minimizing the potential of the people to revolt against a dictatorial system of suppression?

These questions of course are strictly socio-political and therefore outside the limits of a book of business ethics. Nevertheless, and contrary to the belief in hyper-capitalism, according to which businesses should only have economic objectives[11], we believe in something more down to earth and pragmatic: that business has now become part of the unbreakable social

---

[10] Mary Carmichael, A Shot of Hope, pages 43-48, Christian Caryl, Cool, Clear Water, page 49, Emily Flynn Venkat, Reward for Good Behavior, page 50, Bill Gates, Saving the World Is Within Our Grasp, page 51, in *Newsweek,* 1st October 2007, Giving Globally. Furthermore, less than ten years later Gates is considered by *Time,* as one of "the 10 Richest People of All Time," August 1st, 2015. His personal wealth is equivalent to the GNP of whole nations. Do we have here a pronounced case of business ethics and moral responsibility towards the world? Do we assume a new role and ethical command of the business leaders and those who manage wealth?

[11] Robert B. Reich, *Supercapitalism: The Transformation of Business, Democracy and Everyday Life*, Random House, New York 2007; Also, Naomi Klein, *The Shock Doctrine: The Rise of the Disaster Capitalism,* Penguin Books, London, U.K., 2007.

fabric, and thus all businesses have a responsibility to the people, the environment and the future of society.

What is the purpose of this book?

The business organization, like any organized social organization, develops its own «culture». The culture defines ethics business code of conduct and rules of acceptable behavior. For example, what is the proper way to conduct business with a customer? How to treat a worker? What are the corporate responsibilities and obligations towards the owner of capital invested in the firm? What are the corporate responsibilities to the people and to the environment in general? The questions are innumerable and the aim of this book is to give the reader the opportunity to open his mind to new possibilities and to realize that good business sense and ethical behavior should work in tandem. A well-developed business code of ethics will enhance business operations for it will allow corporate stakeholders to understand better the corporate vision, its strategy, its tactics and its objectives and will allow people to share its good aspirations.

At the same time the reader may wish to find in this text a concise and complete reference that will not overburden her time neither will demand advanced knowledge of concepts and methodologies. This text aims to simplify business ethics notions and to present them in a compact and straightforward manner. It is written for students who venture this field for first time, a general audience of "interested" readers, specialized "how-to-do" business ethics seminars and anyone who thinks as an entrepreneur or conducts business. Note that this text does not seek to develop a theory of philosophy or ethics or to predispose the reader towards any particular belief system, or to even enhance ethical behaviors.

However, this text asks questions, raises doubts and lets the reader decide about his personal ethical basis. In an age of information and knowledge, at a time when hundreds of millions of people are experiencing a second life and virtual reality through internet connections, it would be an unrealistic daring to write a book on business ethics in accordance with our personal beliefs. We are simply the cartographers of the readers' journey to allow each person to chart their own self-actualization course according to their own cultural backgrounds and philosophical way of thinking[12]. The present text, in many instances, follows the structure of well-known books on business ethics authored over the last thirty years[13]. Moreover, recognizing that in its classic sense philosophy did not address the specificities of business practice, it aims to (a) outline the evolution of philosophy to ethics as it relates to the 21st century practices, (b) address specific topics of business ethics, (c) relate business ethics to corporate governance and culture-specific realities, and (d) propose a platform assisting the "how-to" structuring of a corporation's business ethics code.

Structure of the book

The book has seven chapters. The first two chapters are on the theory of ethics. The first refers to philosophical and ethical questions, as they have evolved through the centuries and the second is introducing the reader to the realities of our century, an era that (perhaps) forced us to have different approaches, attitudes and ways of thinking and institutions. The two chapters are not seeking to teach philosophy or sociology, just to introduce the reader to some basic concepts used in later chapters.

---

[12] The modern man may be facing primordial stages of experience, for example, from indigenous people living in the Amazon or Australia, to being completely addicted to technological influences of the everyday life.

[13] The authors consider that some of the textbooks on business ethics defined the era of corporate social responsibility; examples: Goodpaster, K. E. and K. M. Sayre, Editors, *Ethics and Problems of the 21st Century*, University of Notre Dame Press, Notre Dame, IN 1979; Beauchamp, Tom L. and Norman E. Bowie, *Ethical Theory in Business*, 5th Edition, Prentice Hall, Upper Saddle River, New Jersey, 1997; Thiroux, Jacques, *Ethics: Theory and Practice*, 6th Edition, Prentice Hall, Upper Saddle River, New Jersey, 1998; Trevino, Linda K. and Katherine A. Nelson, *Managing Business Ethics: Straight Talk About How To Do It Right,* Second Edition, John Wiley and Sons, New York 1999, *Challenges of Corporate Social Responsibility*, The Philip Morris Institute, Brussels, Belgium 2000; Richardson, John E. Editor, *Business Ethics 01/02*, Thirteenth Edition, Annual Editions McGraw-Hill/Dushkin, Guilford, Connecticut 2001; Richard T. DeGeorge, *Business Ethics*, Sixth Edition, Pearson/Prentice Hall, Upper Saddle River, NJ 2006; John R. Boatright, *Ethics and the Conduct of Business*, Fifth Edition, Pearson/Prentice Hall, Upper Saddle River, NJ 2007. Of course, in the recent years many great books exist. It should be noted that the teaching of business ethics started in the 1970s. For a brief overview of the evolution of this teaching, see Tilden J. Curry, Teaching Business Ethics: The Perspective of One Business Dean, Krishna S. Dhir, Editor, *The Dean's Perspective*, Decision Science Institute, Atlanta, Georgia 2008, pages 88-93.

The third chapter focuses on an institutional phenomenon of our era, the corporation. Though the concept existed throughout human existence, it is only during the last one hundred years that took prominence. Presently corporations' annual revenues are often larger than countries gross domestic products and corporations have responsibilities beyond corporate philosophy and ethics, to assist in all fields of human endeavor, including technology, social revitalizing, education, even employee happiness.

The next four chapters address specific issues of business ethics which refer to the business market, customers, funding sources, employees in the company, its owners and its business environment. In addition, at the end, the seventh chapter aims to give «practical advice» on how to set up a code of business ethics.

Beyond the theory, the book is sprinkled with special topics, definitions, views, advices and «box information» in an effort to become as meaningful as possible and pleasant to read, without over theorizing and by presenting a relatively short, but conceptually substantial, text.

Some tips for the teachers of this book

Given our experiences with the previous three (and expanded) editions of this book and since a variety of educators are using this book in their classes, it is customary in academic texts to have a short section of advice from the authors to any who wish to benefit from not so obvious explanations or didactic approaches. Also, instructor's teaching manuals and test banks are offered containing texts from specialized topics to multiple-choice tests. Therefore, this text will be soon followed by another one, *Business Ethics Practices.* Here are a few pointers about this book that we think will help the teaching process. For more information, please contact us at jt@unipi.gr and/or ppetratos@csustan.edu.

Opposite to most recent books on business ethics the present text aims to cover the necessary material in brief chapters of easily readable pages. The text is comprised of seven, about equal in teaching length chapters, which have been developed so that they can be also presented as modules of professional seminars or to be easily read from the general audience. In

"Business Ethics Practices" special topics maybe used to illustrate issues of the chapter's main theme, some of them being real life case studies whereas others having a more specific focus. As already mentioned soon we shall have them available through a separate text "Business Ethics Practices". The instructor may use some of them according to the way she wants to present such issues to her class or use her own articles and/or case studies. In other words her teaching plan should dictate what will be included, according to the available teaching hours.

The material has been extensively used for about fifteen years. The ideal class for this book is introductory undergraduate or graduate class in business ethics and corporate governance, size thirty to forty-five persons, taught three hours a time, once a week, for eleven weeks (including exam periods). Although we think that the ideal class size is 30-45 students, still there were very positive experiences teaching first-year students in classes of 150 students taking the course as required, or in highly demanding graduate classrooms with 15-25 people, taking the class as an elective.

Please note that we saw impressive results when creating working groups, preferably teams of five, thus creating a sense of duty for being present and involved at every meeting and sitting at the same location and lighting a spirit of active learning and team building[14]. Also, we recommend

---

[14] Active learning is a teaching approach where in each lesson the professor chooses a series of issues covering the class material. Such issues are presented at the end of this text at the section "Some of the business ethics issues raised …" The class has been already split in semester-long teams and appropriate answering forms are distributed. Then, the professor, per his teaching plan, poses a question to the class. For two minutes every student tries to think of an answer and writes down a casual reply, using data from the text, general knowledge matter, or the press. During those two minutes there is no debate or discussion between team members. After almost four minutes discussion in groups the team leader writes down the response they consider more appropriate to the question. Randomly groups are selected to develop positions or to refute the positions earlier stated by another team. Then the response forms are collected for grading and the teacher goes on to the next item. For use in large classes, we recommend the approach outlined in: "Teaching International Business in ' Mega '- Classes ", at the 2007 Annual meeting of the Association for Global Business, November 15-18 in Washington, DC, in Robert J. Keating, Editor, Proceedings of the 2007 Conference of the Association for Global Business, a cd-rom and "Teaching International Business in 'Mega' Classes: A Case Study," *Journal of Teaching in International Business*, Volume 15 (Number 3), 2004, pages 61-76.). This approach proved to be very appropriate for teaching business ethics, both in academic and business environments, whereas for specialized graduate

reading the footnotes. Some of these are of great interest and have different perspectives which, if they were in the text, might have negatively affected the flow of the subject matter. Finally, for those of our colleagues that are in tune of using active learning and/or seek discussion platforms on topics related to business ethics, please visit at the end of this volume "Some of the business ethics issues raised…..". The topics have been analyzed at the respective pages and we have them very appropriate for active learning, small class presentations, team building and/or short student compositions.

Acknowledgments

Firstly, we would like to thank all our colleagues, academic teachers, researchers, business executives, trade unionists, environmentalists, lawyers, and many others who contributed to the creation of the foundations of business ethics.

Their combined efforts brought to the world in very few years, an extraordinary international awareness of business ethics as well as corporate governance, which essentially changes older ways of thinking and implementing global business. It is an excellent contribution especially appreciated in subsequent generations. They are the architects of very major societal changes.

In particular, for the book you hold in your hands we wish to thank everyone who has helped in its previous editions, all of them in Greek. They are too many to mention by name without the risk to miss anyone. Nevertheless, and though many of them are now deceased, we would like

---

audiences in-depth understanding of philosophy, theology, cosmos and individual self-actualization perspectives are addressed (See John Thanopoulos "How to Add Philosophy Dimensions in Your Basic International Business Course," *Journal of Teaching in International Business*, Volume 21 (Issue 3), July-September 2010, pages 189-199, and John Thanopoulos, *The Global Manager: Self- actualization Perspectives*, coauthored with 185 of his Fall 2009 students, first electronic edition (cd-rom), Interbooks, Athens 2010. More recently, similar concepts appear in John Thanopoulos "Insights from Teaching International Business in 'Mega" Classes" at the 2014, 26th annual meeting of the Association for Global Business, November 13-15, 2014, in Orlando, Florida in Charles M. Byles, Editor, *AGB and IALBSS Proceedings of the 2014 Conference*, on cd-rom.

particularly to thank Jim Dunlap, Theofanis Tsoulouhas, Keith Whitfield, Raymond Torto, Chris Boosalis, David Lindsay, George Minettas, L. L. Schkade, Evan Syrigos, Phil Taylor, Willis Wolf, Zbigniew Gackowski, Pi-Sheng Deng, Al Tsacle, Pengtao Li, Gregory Papanikos, Panayiotis Ziridis. Moreover, we wish to express our heartfelt "thank you" to our thousands of students: We, teachers, are learning more from them than we actually teach them … and in matters as those of this text *they* led our thinking to the needs of the social future.

Certainly, for any errors remaining, we are personally responsible.

John Thanopoulos, Panagiotis Petratos,
January 2016

CHAPTER 1

FROM PHILOSOPHY TO ETHICS

What you will learn in this Chapter

In this chapter you will learn ...

- Definitions and thoughts on what is ethics and business ethics.
- Definitions and thoughts on what is philosophy.
- Definitions and thoughts on what is 'true'.
- About the basic 'schools' ethics.
- About the relationship of philosophy, ethics, and business ethics.
- About the information era and its impact on the culture of philosophy and ethics.
- About the methodology of ethics investigation.
- About the perception of corruption.
- About the ethics literature.
- About the legal versus the ethics argument.
- About information technology and related philosophical perspectives.
- About ethics and self-actualization.

Introduction to Chapter 1

This chapter gives the reader an idea of the basic concepts of philosophy and business ethics. In this chapter we begin by giving the definitions of ethics, business ethics and ethical code of business conduct. These explanations are necessary to introduce the novice reader to the tone of this book. Next we explain the associations of the concepts of ethics, business ethics, code of business conduct and give a basic idea of the concepts of "truth" and philosophy. We also discuss the research methodology of ethics scholars, the basic "schools" of thought relevant to our business ethics analysis and point to how the ethical business issues relate to business facts, figures and profits. For example, accounting expertise and electronic technology have assisted business tax evasion, employees' pension contribution which is legal but not necessarily ethical business.

The next chapter refers to the realities of our time. In the last fifty years, major social mutations occurred due to the catalysts of the electronic age, technology, and globalization. New social realities and moral foundations could not have been foreseen in the time of Plato, Kant or Leibniz. The population of our planet doubled in the last 30 years, the speed of propagation of information has increased by leaps and bounds, and dramatic changes have taken place in key institutions and in the establishment of global, international business. All these facts compel us to do an overview of social trends, as we see them today. The second chapter is followed by a chapter focusing on the corporation which will take the role of the major institutional player of the 21st century. Then, there are four chapters that discuss the ethics of the stakeholders of the enterprise. Therefore, this chapter is the philosophical base that connects us to the next chapters which mainly relate to positions of business ethics.

Ethics and business

For millennia, cultures have developed philosophies based on geographic and spatial realities they faced, the individual, family, the 'race' were the key elements of any society. Over the years, socio-cultural developments, historical necessities, wars, transnational influences and technological advances further adjusted the philosophical foundation of cultures which had to be developed on distinct philosophical-ethical bases along with their respective legal forms.

Therefore, it sounds logical that the philosophy and ethics of a people in a locale is inextricably connected with the geographic, socio-cultural, economic, historical and temporal context. Let us start from the beginning. What is ethics?

- Ethics is the branch of philosophy dealing with values relating to human behavior with regard to the fairness or inappropriateness of acts, the goodness or evilness of motive or aim.
- Ethics is the set of lessons of any religion, ideology or doctrinal beliefs that determine what is good and what is bad or what is allowed and what is not permitted in a specific social context.

- Ethics is a constantly evolving set of rules for human behavior that characterizes a social group during a particular era.
- Ethics (after Greek *τά ἠθικά*) is the science of morals concerned with the principles of human duty[15].

Though we shall return to these definitions, the reader is cautioned that they present a static inflexibility. They present what is "ethics" in this current moment during the time of analysis, given the accepted cultural norms. But what about the ethical and moral behaviors in business and society throughout time? We can remedy this definitional vacuum by adding a statement explaining that ethics deals with how people treat other people and other beings in order to promote the public interest, progress, creativity, sense of good and evil, fair or unfair[16]. In our opinion, it is necessary to define clearly what is ethical but also to understand and promote social and business affairs of any given cultural specificity. As we will see in Chapter 3, the major institutional player is the corporation which nowadays functions in a global business village.

We are born within a set of rules of conduct and from the beginning, we are taught to obey these rules and avoid the unpleasant consequences of failing to follow them. We are rewarded to follow instructions and obey rules. Different principles of conduct govern a strict Muslim living and

---

[15] These definitions were sourced, although some have been amended from the work of *Oxford Dictionary of English Language*, Oxford University Press, Har/Cdr edition November 16, 2009. For the interested reader, more are addressed as follows:
1602   W. Warner Epitome Hist. Eng. in Albions Eng. (rev. ed.) xii. lxxv. 313   Nor wanted thear..that did relye On Physickes and on Ethickes, and..a God deny.
1677   I. Barrow Serm. Several Occasions (1678) 195   Out of them [sc. St. Paul's epistles] might well be compiled a Body of Ethicks, or System of Precepts de officiis.
1691   A. Wood Athenæ Oxonienses I. 258   He was made Professor of Eloquence and Ethicks in the Universitie of Ingolstade.
1693   Dryden Disc. conc. Satire in tr. Juvenal Satires p. xxxiii,   The Stoick [philosophy]: The most noble, most generous..amongst all the Sects, who have given us the Rules of Ethiques.
1789   J. Bentham Introd. Princ. Morals & Legisl. xix. §11   Ethics at large may be defined, the art of directing men's actions to the production of the greatest possible quantity of happiness.
1836   R. W. Emerson Nature vi. 72   Ethics and religion differ herein; that the one is the system of human duties commencing from man; the other, from God.
1889   W. B. Carpenter Bampton Lect. vii,   Religion without ethics seems little else than irreligious religion.
[16] See Jacques Thiroux, *Ethics: Theory and Practice*, 6th Edition, Prentice Hall, Upper Saddle River, New Jersey, 1998, page 28.

working in a traditional rural area of North Yemen from a Christian living in Monte Carlo and working in the casino. Different principles of conduct govern an American from Africa and his parents and grandparents, who like him, grew up in a ghetto in Chicago, from the young person who grew up in luxurious beach villas in southern France and belongs to a genealogical tree with enormous trust funds, estates and wealth and her parents and grandparents have always followed a family tradition to perpetually aim to increase their wealth in the US stock market whilst sailing in their yachts in the French Riviera.

With simplicity Apostle Paul explains this lifestyle difference, saying that the rules of conduct we have, just like a set of consciousness codes, are written in our hearts[17]. Therefore, and to a great extent, when we come to this world as we find an already-formed language, which we gradually learn to use, so we find an already established ethics code, a system of moral rules, which we gradually become accustomed to follow and learn to respect and keep them.

After the Second World War, another factor, beyond the individual, family and "race" begins to play a central role. This element, which in various forms has re-occurred in the most primitive human societies, is the business venture. In this context business venture means the collection of human initiatives through which a specific aim is achieved. A business venture includes clearly expressed procedures, the combination of various essential resources and factors of production, risk taking and meeting production requirements and peoples' needs. Business ventures created the Parthenon, aspirin, or the first sewing machine.

In the 21st century elements which continue to play a significant role include the individuals, institutions like the family, and countries. However business, especially international business, starts to become the key means of social progress, technological development, inter-country balance, education, and change. As in earlier times a properly consensus-crafted and continuously adjusted legal framework is a pre-requirement of an acceptable set of rules by the mainstream of society. Thus, alongside the modern enterprise we must have socially accepted open and fair procedures, or rather, business ethics formulated consistently with social compatibility. As we will see in Chapter 7, the code of business ethics

---

[17] See the Epistle of Apostle Paul to the Romans, Chapter II, verses 14-16.

springs from the environment of the company, which also defines key principles of corporate governance and, therefore, its social responsibility.

> Answering the question of a student, the Chairman of the U.S. Federal Reserve Board, Alan Greenspan, said: "The best chance you have of making a big success in this world is to decide from square one that you are going to do it ethically ". This answer was given in an interview after the Enron Award for Distinguished Public Service was conferred to Alan Greenspan, on November 13, 2001. Note that a few days before the award, the business leaders of Enron, one of the biggest US corporations, had already been proven responsible of major wrongful administrative irregularities, but the prize was given through the James A. Baker Institute of Public Affairs and had been announced significantly earlier[18].

What is philosophy, what is truth?

In the previous section we saw that ethos, the term that directly concerns us, particularly in relation to the business enterprise, is a branch of philosophy. How we defined the term philosophy? Leading scholars would tell us that philosophy, a composite Hellenic word that relates the concepts of friendship and wisdom, is[19]:

- The logical investigation and search of the nature of things and the truth of beings and phenomena, knowledge and values.

- The systematic review of the scientific world which also shapes industry.

- The theory or set of ideas which form the basis of a particular subject matter or activity, and so on.

So philosophy is the search for truth, at various levels and in view of specific perspectives. Philosophy was conceived and developed not always in the same way. There is a general search for truth. It began as an

---

[18] See The Rule of Allan Sloan and Michael Isikoff, The Enron Effect, *Newsweek*, 28 January 2002, page 40.
[19] Philosophy. (2013). In *Encyclopædia Britannica*. Retrieved from http://www.britannica.com/EBchecked/topic/456811/philosophy

effort to better understand the world (pre-Socratic philosophers), developed as ethics (Socrates), then as metaphysics (Plato) and in modern times has taken many other directions. It is the logical investigation and search of the nature of things and the truth of beings and phenomena, knowledge and values. It is the systematic examination of the world and disciplines shaped by humanity. It is the theory or set of ideas which form the basis of a particular subject matter or activity. So let's see what is truth or in Hellenic "αλήθεια". "Αλήθεια" is a composite Hellenic word that composes together the privative "α" which means un- and "λήθη" oblivion to create a new word un-oblivion. So the reader in this light may say that truth is a reference to events or things that are not forgotten and are always true. The reader may accept a more specific definition. Thus, truth is:

- Everything which is in line with the facts, to the reality, what actually happened or is happening or is absolutely certain to happen.

- The full report of individual episodes that make up an event without concealment or misrepresentation of data, with a presentation based on a scientifically valid methodology.

- What agrees with common sense in a specific place and time.

- What can be verified experimentally and so on.

"What is truth" was the question that Pontius Pilate asked Jesus, had pondered the ancient philosophers, we continue to wonder today, and the question will probably continue forever. In October 2000, the magazine *Forbes-ASAP*, published a special edition titled, "What Is True?" and asked some of the important business thinkers of our time to express their opinion about what is true. Here are some of these thoughts[20]:

- "Early on, I was attracted to the technology business because I really thought it represented an inner circle of understanding." … "Everything is changing, and change is good." Speed is the key to understanding information; speed changes the meaning of

---

[20] What Is True? ", *Forbes-ASAP*, 2 October 2000, pages 37, 47, 49, 50, 57, 73, 74, 237, 273. Quotes have been partially adapted to fit the purposes of this text.

information." "The speed of the message is the message." … "Technology makes the weak strong."

- "The truth can be elusive, or at least difficult to express in the business world. So, I find myself turning to metaphors and analogies, borrowing images from sports or even war to drive home my business strategy and motivate the troops. …. Four decades into the digital revolution, we live in a world where every sound and image can be manipulated by computers which makes the potential for deception quite high …"

- "We live in the 'Age of Falsification" filled with surfaces that we cannot trust. Some are digital creations ... We cannot believe everything we see, hear or read because what we see, hear and read are contradictory and potentially false. Even our senses can deceive us."

- "Within this new world of human, economic and technological relationships, many people are struggling for a metaphor that will give us a sense of where we are now. ... Will we become no more than versions of that Frankenstein monster, our thoughts and appetites stitched together by the commercial culture, making us even more lonely, leaving us to grow more and more desperate in our sense for camaraderie, companionship, empathy, love, and authenticity?"

- "As the basic institution or wealth creation, the corporation is undergoing profound change. ... People can increase wealth by adding the value of knowledge to a product or service, through innovation, enhancement, cost reduction or customization. This new network is giving companies the far reaching ability to create value and generate wealth, or acquire what I call the digital capital."

- "Injustice undermines the truth, and without truth there can be no lasting peace..."

- There is no absolute truth. You are committing an act of personal faith when you claim that the scientific method, including mathematics and logic, is the privileged road to the truth.

Let us review a summary of considerations before proceeding. How to act appropriately for a modern enterprise depends on the principles of business ethics that have been adopted. These principles stem from a general ethical framework that the business owners, employees, customers and others associated with the enterprise have adopted as acceptable evidence of the set of rules valued by society. This context of ethics is described by a broader philosophical acceptance. A central part of any philosophy is to try to discover the truth. The questions posed by the above modern thinkers, are very small sample searches for the truth and are part of an effort that lasted for millennia, since the first existence of humankind. These are a potpourri of concerns of how we see these philosophical issues today compared to the same questions that Plato and Pericles and Kant tried to answer earlier.

> "In the business world we want results. One of the greatest temptations is to do whatever it takes to get those results, even if that involves shamelessly manipulating other people. And of course, the way we manipulate other people is primarily manipulating the truth, by bluffing, by a little deception, by lying." ….
>
> Tom Morris[21]

Modern technology seems to play an important role in the formulation of truth. In principle, technology enables us to investigate the truth, the formulation of the present. For example, 2,000 years ago from our place of work we could not order specific information to come immediately before us, even if we had the power of life and death over millions of people and commanded entire empires like Cesar. Today, the Internet avails all kinds of information to every connected user with the entry of simple keywords

---

[21] Tom Morris, *If Aristotle Ran General Motors: The New Soul of Business*, Henry Holt and Company, New York 1997, pages 39 και 44. Quotes have been partially adapted to fit the purposes of this text.

(we can search multiple data bases via key-words.) We can bring within seconds directly to our desk thousands of topics to analyze. Today, via computers, we can author a complex analysis study, create an impressive presentation and send it where ever we wish. Let us remember that after the invention of printing no human is employed as a manual hand writing copyist and that only very recently technology has enabled a wide scale electronic data transmission. Today, through mass media we can see an event within minutes from the time it happened, such as the crash of planes in the towers in New York, or to hear about an avalanche or a tsunami heading to us.

But the technology itself creates barriers to our sense of truth. In the past people relied on personal observations and their senses to discover and formulate arguments. Staying for years in the same place they studied the stars, plants, and people with admirable accuracy, confirming the existence or absence of the subject of study by sight, touch, smell. Now, the "technological man"-let us call him/her ... homo technologicus- can create fictitious pictures and bring before us, even in dematerialized form, a dinosaur, the Titanic, or a global video-conferencing event, with convincing, sound and vision (researchers are still working on the digital propagation of scents). Homo Technologicus can "wear" prosthetics to make him/her more powerful, may appear simultaneously in front of billions of people, can inform and misinform, can claim something as true, and because of the strong power of communication he/she possesses can start a war. Here again comes to mind the need to define the limits of good and evil, truth and untruth, ethical and unethical. Therefore, one should question the distinction between good and evil, true and untrue, which, to a great extend should be assessed as inevitably pragmatic. Real can only be the distinction between the existential authenticity of truth from the existential alienation of fiction.[22]

The considerations above give us a different sense for the truth. As it is evident humans are not relying on the original concept of senses and consciousness anymore to establish the truth, logic, philosophy. Therefore, let us start from the beginning...

---

[22] Christos Yiannaras, *The decline as a challenge*, A.A. Libani, Athens 1999, page 276.

We have to examine how truth is written in business? Through an accounting methodology! For the majority of the people, accounting thought inspires objectivity and credibility. Is this true? Hundreds of thousands of doctoral dissertations and articles are written on contemporary accounting subjects. It makes sense to have a single and unique method of systematic accounting thought? Probably not.[23] Moreover, the complexity of contemporary accounting makes it difficult for small shareholders of a company who may not realize how the company performs, to understand what is meant by "indicators", and what are the risks of the new company ventures for the pension and retirement of small shareholders who invested their life savings for their old age.

Perhaps the most shocking example of a series of modern accounting irregularities, suspect practices and unethical activities is Enron, once the 7th largest U.S. Corporation. Following disclosures by the Vice President, former accountant of a large accounting firm Arthur Andersen, Sherron S. Watkins, Enron went bankrupt. It should be noted that the official directors of Enron and accountants from the offices of Arthur Andersen in Houston, Texas, were found to be responsible for the majority of accounting irregularities that took place[24]. Watkins in her letter to the director of Enron, Kenneth L. Lay, wrote that the company is threatened to implode in a wave of accounting scandals[25].

The study of ethics

In previous sections we gave some definitions about philosophy and some position statements about truth. But what is ethics? A standard dictionary

---

[23] For comparative accounting and international accounting rules and ethics, see Thanopoulos, *Global Business and Corporate Governance: Environment, Structure and Challenges,* New York, Business Expert Press 2014, pages 95-111.

[24] See Mike McNamee, Amy Borus and Christopher Palmeri, Out of Control at Andersen, *BusinessWeek*, April 8, 2002, pages 78-79.

[25] Zellner, Wendy and Stephanie Forest Anderson, A Hero-and a smoking-gun letter, page 42, *BusinessWeek*, January 28, 2002. And also see articles in the same edition: Bruce Nussbaum, Can you trust anybody anymore, pages 39-40, and Joseph Weber, et al., Can Andersen survive, pages 46-47, and Byrnes, Nanette, et al., Accounting in crisis, pages 50-54.

defines ethics as the "principles of morality, or the field of study of morals or right conduct; a particular ethical system; the rules of conduct recognized in respect to a particular class of human actions;" and so on[26]. We may say, therefore, that ethics is the branch of philosophy dealing with values that are related to human behavior with regard to the appropriateness or inappropriateness of acts, their goodness or not, their motives or their purpose.

Each religion, ideology or belief system offers principles that determine what is good and what is bad or what is allowed and what is not allowed in a specific social context. This is a constantly evolving set of rules for human behavior that characterizes a social group, during a particular time period. This set of rules is indicative of the principles and values that a person should develop and maintain in his everyday life.

On a more practical basis, ethics deals with how people treat other people and other beings in order to promote everyone's well-being, public interest, progress, creativity, sense of good and evil, fair or unfair.

Based on these definitions, and always within the same social context and time period, we can define a person as ethical, in the case that her behavior is consistent with the accepted ethical laws or unethical if her behavior deviates from the accepted norm. Could someone argue that ethical values are not firmly supported by social foundations? Then such a person could deny the validity of ethical laws, deny the distinction between good and evil, and accept a lifestyle that is governed by release of morals and shameless conduct. We would not say this person is unethical, we would say this person is amoral (or immoral), indifferent to moral responsibility, we may say independent of moral distinctions. In other words, the unethical person knowingly violates the moral law whereas the amoral violates the moral law unconsciously because she has no moral conscience.

---

[26] *(The) Lexicon Webster Dictionary*, Volume I, The English-Language Institute of America, Inc. 1977, page 337.

The definitions presented above require the very existence of a methodology to explore the concepts of moral and ethical laws. We can approach the analysis of ethics in two ways.

Scientific or descriptive approach

Here the emphasis is on empirical observation, an approach used in social sciences, and based on accepted scientific methodologies. For example, a researcher of human psychology observes a carefully selected group of people with predetermined characteristics for certain behaviors under certain conditions, and compares with a similar sample that has different control variable(s) to collect, observe and compare experimental evidence. Researchers note that their findings draw conclusions about the behavior of the samples used, but add their own assessments of what is right or not, or how these people should behave..

Philosophical approach

This dimension adds to our own scientific understanding of what must be the way forward. There is no longer only one single objective scientific approach. The analyst makes a norm, a rule of conduct. For example, the analyst can reach the following conclusion based on observation of the majority of population: "Based on the findings of our study, people are selfish and act selfishly". Therefore it is expected, and this depends on the beliefs and persuasion of reason capable people, to create schools and spheres of influence in the formulation of what is ethical, and what are the role models of objective values.

In essence, the philosophical approach has a different dynamic. While some may base their philosophical system on the existence of a supernatural power, for example, Allah, the Twelve Gods, the Infinite, Jesus, others may believe that ethics is an extension of physical laws. It is remarkable that Einstein said that he did not believe in the ethical person and that he understood the world of ethics as purely a human construct without any supernatural basis[27].

---

[27] Mark Winocur, *Einstein, A Portrait, Pomegranate Artbooks*, Corte-Madera, CA, page 96. The reference is found in Jacques Thiroux, *Ethics: Theory and Practice*, 6th Edition,

Study of ethics and its scientific or philosophical approach are major human approaches in understanding them. However, we should also examine the implementation potential and the realities of our world where proposed beliefs will flourish. Archbishop Desmond Tutu, a Nobel peace laureate whose rebellious leadership in his forties has soften thirty years later, and carrying his life-long experience, admits that the texture of our universe is one where there is no question at all but that good, laughter and justice will prevail[28]. Positions as his produce not only strategic philosophical and ethical perceptions like good and justice, but also social implementation practical instruments, like laughter or tolerance.

An ethical dimension of the social sciences theory: Corruption

The previous subsection discussed the scientific or philosophical investigation and descriptive approach, a methodology adapted to the social research. Let us discuss it through the following research effort:

In discussing the concept of ethics, we find the term "corruption" that has been the subject of many social studies, usually in analyzing human behavior or in the dynamic relationship between "major player" and "customer". Social science conclusions are based on acceptance or rejection of cases which we analyze with accepted statistical tools. Examples:

* Higher corruption is associated with lower per capita income,
* Higher corruption is associated with less economic freedom,
* Higher corruption is associated with lower quality of bureaucracy,
* Higher corruption is associated with higher political instability,
* Higher corruption is associated with higher social distancing,
* Higher corruption is associated with a higher tendency to avoid uncertainty.

To proceed, we must be able to fully understand the variables which will enable us, using appropriate statistical tools, to arrive to the above

Prentice Hall, Upper Saddle River, New Jersey, on page 33. The same source was used to develop previously arguments on empirical issues and philosophical approaches.
[28] Alex Perry and Catherine Mayer, The Laughing Bishop, *Time*, October 11, 2010, page 30.

associations. Case in point is the term corruption which can be evaluated using the Corruption Perception Index (CPI), assuming that as researchers we conceptually agree with definitions, hypotheses, sample bases, and testing procedures. By parallel reasoning, we use the variables economic freedom, quality of bureaucracy, political instability, social –power-distancing, tendency to avoid uncertainty and the corresponding variables of economic freedom[29].

In fact, it is the aim of Hoon Park's work[30] to reach conclusions on the previous statements about corruption or the costs that corruption incurs in the business economy, an even more complicated analysis effort than more standardized research approaches[31]. Therefore, it is necessary for the reader to understand not only the statistical methodology social research requires, but also to have a deeper knowledge of the research timing, the framework of analysis, the potential autocorrelation of the variables involved, the cultural specificity and the ethical complexity of the research effort[32].

School of ethics

Our thoughts and the formulation of theories are the result of the environment we grew up. In a different light we shall see the world and the ethical principles as a Buddhist monk and in different light as a cannibal anthropophagus man-eater warrior. The paragraphs that follow are based on the logic of American, European and Hellenic perspectives.

---

[29] These variables available to us from sources such as Transparency International, Economist Intelligence Unit, National Statistics and accepted previous investigations have suggested terms such as Hofstede terms power distance, uncertainty avoidance, masculinity and cultural collectivism. See also Geert Hofstede, National cultures in four dimensions, *International Studies of Management and Organization*, 1983, pages 46-74.
[30] Hoon Park presented at the 2002 conference of the Association for Global Business findings on the issue of corruption through the work of the Determinants of Corruption: A Cross-national Analysis, where he elaborated on the previous cases.
[31] For example, such research, see M. Anaam Hashmi and Faramarz Damanpour, Cost of Corruption and Implications for MNCs: Special Focus on South Asia, *The Journal of Current Research in Global Business*, Fall 2002, pages 39-47.
[32] For example, studies of the same period show negative results when there is corruption in foreign direct investment both for the recipient and the country of origin, as that corruption may create operational problems in cases of FDI. Moshin Habib and Leon Zurawicki, (2002) Corruption and Foreign Direct Investment, Journal of International Business Studies, Volume 33, No 2, Second Quarter 2002, pages 291-307. A further analysis of such topics may distract the attention of the reader from the main arguments of this section.

Let's start with a purely hypothetical example. A group of Greek businessmen visit Las Vegas in Nevada USA. They are impressed with the fact that in the desert, and initially starting only a few decades years ago, some visionary entrepreneurs capitalized on the existence of some hotels, entertainment centers and corruption that existed there and developed one of the major convention centers in the world, with all the prerequisites and rewards of such an effort. Las Vegas is a place which can accommodate hundreds of thousands of people with hotels, restaurants, casinos, entertainment of all kinds, conference facilities, a large airport, and much, much, more, needed to support a city of this scale.

The idea of hypothetical visitors to Las Vegas is that national interest in Greece is increasing to implement a parallel idea. Moreover, Greece has a much better climate, more natural beauty many archaeological antiquities and is the birth place of western civilization. Such a plan can thus be projected as the airplane is carrying them back, using foreign capital, to raise the Greek GDP by at least 30%, giving thousands of new jobs, enhancing the quality of Greek tourism and more. The success of such an undertaking would balance any social and economic incompatibilities with the Greek reality, entering new dimensions to the acceptance of this new development as ethically suitable including accepting imperialism of a foreign influence to the Greek tradition and culture, even using a large Greek island for this purpose.

In our example we have two of the most basic aspects of theories on ethics. One considers the purposes, the results and the final consequences of our actions. Indeed, as one theory examines consequences and the other theory does not, the theories are respectively called consequentialist (teleological) and non-consequentialist (deontological). Success justifies the means used. This is called teleological ethics and teleological approach. At the other extreme are approaches of ethical bases. Here the approach of all must be consistent with accepted ethical law which must be followed in each step[33].

[33] For the reader interested in expanding their knowledge of the issue, we recommend the study of Chapters 2 and 3 of the book by John Boatright, *Ethics and the Conduct of Business*, Fourth Edition, Prentice Hall, Upper Saddle River, New Jersey 2003.

Using a teleological ethical basis

One of the most basic subdivisions of the teleological approach called ethical egoism can have one of the following forms:[34]

- "everyone has to act in my interest"
- "I, as a person must act in my interest, but I can't tell others what to do"
- "everyone has to act in her own interest, regardless of the interests of others, unless the interests of others coincide with her own"

Is the business, as such, ethical or not? It is interesting to hear how one can see the business venture from the Christian viewpoint. "... Lost behind significant prejudices and political, ideological exploitation, the Christian truth about business was lost as expressly stated in the official church documents, with joint responsibility of ecclesiastical authorities, who by ignorance and conservative placement, attempt to keep the myth and keep the evangelical true official version. The evangelist Matthew mentions the parable in which Jesus interpreted the duty of man to attempt business, reaching eternal damnation after refusing business aiming to the return of goods and gifts and having won the most by business. ...denial of the business under any ideology is of evil origin and proof of laziness, therefore, in the Christian view, is a sin, i.e. departure from the divine will. Multiplying the profit of the business is justified, after a person who has the soundest of intentions attempts greater profitability and will be reimbursed by the rewards he deserves as well as the missed opportunity profits of the lazy who avoided business. Put simply, justified is the man who tries, who exploits all the possibilities, free will and logic offer to him and from this process gains the most. This is the person who uses correctly God given privileges of nature."

Konstantinos Papanikolaou, journalist, Archimandrite[35]

Theories of the ethical egoism first appeared during the time of the ancient Greek philosopher Epikouros, 341 – 270 bC. It is reasonable to have many

---

[34] Op. Cit., Thiroux, pages 38-43.

[35] Translation of parts of his speech at the University of Piraeus, 18 December 2001. The speech was entitled: The ethics of business in Western societies. Christian perception and distortion.

academic disputes on the above positions, although philosophers were known supporters of them even during our modern history[36].

For example, Epikouros stated "it is impossible to live a pleasant life without living wisely and well and justly and it is impossible to live wisely and well and justly without living a pleasant life." Epikouros' philosophy is the earliest in Ancient Greece to express the foundational and essential ideas of Ethics. Ethics based on Epikouros' philosophy is a set of rules established on the bases of human fellowship and reciprocity. According to Epikouros' philosophy an individual's well-being is the community's well-being and they are both dependent upon people's fair and just actions, which do no harm to oneself and to fellow humans, therefore maximizing a pleasant life and happiness for all.

Another teleological "school" appeared in the 18th century by Jeremy Betham and the 19th century by John Stuart Mill, which is geared towards an approach of community service or utilitarian nature (utilitarianism), although again it could be argued that similar considerations were philosophized from antiquity.

Unfortunately, especially in our modern times of extreme materialism, widespread profusion and luxury epidemic some people who are driven by hyper-consumption have distorted this philosophy to a more unimaginative and uninspired meaning to fit their prosaist and hedonistic life style. Their interpretation places above all material consumption and pursuit of pleasures as the ultimate quest of life.

All the above express greed in all its forms. Naturally, greed is not the exclusive privilege of the wealthy. Manifestations of greed take different forms depending on the individual's motive and the object of one's desire. The object of one's desire may ignite such a strong impulse that it may very well become the ultimate goal of one's life. In such a state of mind the satisfaction of the individual's need becomes like a quest of cacoethes unquenchable thirst. The object of one's desire becomes like a mirage of an oasis in the desert, which as soon as the person approaches close to it suddenly it disappears like a hallucination and the cycle begins again and the individual goes after the next oasis in a never ending, relentless pursuit.

---

[36] For example, see Ayn Rand, *The Virtue of Selfishness*, New American Library, New York 1964, pages 57-67.

For instance, some individuals feel strongly the urge for acquiring wealth, others have a burning desire to become beautiful, some are keen on becoming powerful, quite a few others feel the need to become famous and many desire all the above. Even since antiquity, philosophical views addressing these issues have been expressed by philosophers.

Greed is also a human characteristic exhibited by people of the arts and letters. For instance, Newton and Leibniz fiercely argued over who was the first to offer to the world the foundations of calculus[37]. In that respect, the approach chosen by the following examples of scientist-leaders is unorthodox and unpopular but more humble, honest and ethical and should be the shining example for all business leaders.

Dr. Grigory Perelman is a mathematician who in 2002 published on the Internet his proof of Poincare's conjecture which is an extremely complex geometrical problem. Ensuing this no small feat Dr. Perelman was awarded the Fields Medal which is equivalent to the Nobel prize for mathematics. He was the first mathematician to refuse the prize because he simply believes that the ideas are what matter and not the individual who conceives them. The duty of that individual is to enlighten and offer his ideas to the world. To make matters more complicated, another very famous mathematician with two of his students also attempted to claim the same proof. Dr. Perelman was disappointed with the ethical standards of the mathematics community but instead of starting a feud like Newton and Leibniz he preferred to keep himself above such insignificant, uninspired and trivial feudal matters[38].

Dr. Jonas Salk is another valiant example of a scientist with a noble cause who developed the vaccine for Poliomyelitis without seeking any business profit for himself whilst offering to the world for free the cure to a very deadly disease as a service to his fellow humans. When a reporter asked him who owns the patent on this vaccine Dr. Salk very simply answered "There is no patent. Could you patent the sun?"[39].

---

[37] *Philosophers at War: The Quarrel Between Newton and Leibniz* by Alfred Rupert Hall, Cambridge University Press. Retrieved from books.google.gr/books?isbn=052152489X.
[38] Source: Sylvia Nasar and David Gruber, Annals of Mathematics, Manifold Destiny A legendary problem and the battle over who solved it,
http://www.newyorker.com/archive/2006/08/28/060828fa_fact2, *The New Yorker*, August 28, 2006,
[39] Breakthrough: the saga of Jonas Salk, by Richard Carter Trident Press. Retrieved from books.google.gr/books?id=69RrAAAAMAAJ.

1941 Nobel Prize Laureate Alexander Fleming is another bright example of a scientist who developed the antibiotic penicillin without any personal business profit. Penicillin is considered one of the most important discoveries of the millennium as it saved millions of lives and was the first of the antibiotics medications.

The human kind needs more business leaders to follow these scientist leaders' ethical examples of selfless contributions to the community for the well-being of our fellow humans, with a sense of self-knowledge and with sharp ethical standards in the business world. Quoting Plato an ancient Greek philosopher, and as it was written over the Delphi temple where Pythia the prophetess of Apollo foresaw the future through oracles "Know Yourself" is a valuable business motto. If an individual achieves self-knowledge then it is much easier for that individual to know his and her contributing role in family, work, community, business and society. If all business leaders knew themselves and their contributing role in society this would be a very different world.

The community service approach stipulates that an action can be ethical if it results in a desirable or good outcome for the community. Therefore, since business objectives and direct pursuit of progress are key elements in society, perhaps, a thorough study of the effects and the expression of ethical procedures could delay or stop a good job. In theory, an action is ethical if ...[40]:

- ... produces the greatest good for most people.
- ... the net gain, after deducting the costs, is maximized for the population as a whole instead of the autocrat, the oligarchy, or any alternative combination.
- ... the immediate and future benefits are maximized for each person even if these benefits outweigh other options.

In modern history, the most striking example of teleological thinking is at the end of the 2nd World War. The atomic bombs that fell on Hiroshima and Nagasaki were decisive at the end of the bloodiest war that humanity has experienced. The two bombs quickly brought the desired result. But there are always many other ethical questions like questions related to the overall impact which in advance could not be calculated.

---

[40] Weiss, Joseph W., *Business Ethics: A Stakeholder and Issues Management Approach*, 3rd Edition, Thomson-South-Western, Mason, Ohio 2003, page 8.

At this point we should refer to ethics as it relates to the concept of rights and the discussion of the theory of utilitarianism[41]. The obvious meaning of today's "right" was not always granted. The slaves had no rights. Only in the last two hundred and thirty years in constitutions like the USA we have human rights such as life, liberty or the pursuit of happiness. Only in 1962, for the first time an official mouth, John F. Kennedy, spoke about consumer rights. Only in 1999, the then UN Secretary-General reported to the Global Compact principles and dependent rights.

It is remarkable that a key religious statement on human rights and ethics for many religions is the golden rule of ethics, "do to others what they will want to do to you", found in every major religion in the world[42]. Perhaps, because there was always the human appeal of the oppression of other people for personal interest the world religions had a duty to make this rule. They were the makers of the main social principles.

For the modern business, although the organizational objectives are teleological, assuming a continuously greater social role, it is required to reassess business approaches. The vast majority of managers do not understand all these business obligations. In addition, observe that "business power" is not always compatible with the concept of business ethics, often oppressing man, for strictly business benefits.

Using a deontological ethical basis

Hence approaches founded on a deontological ethical basis exist in our subconscious sense of what is ethical, or our faith that some higher, divine authority determines the ethical basis of our thinking.

Immanuel Kant linked the logic and ethics and developed a system of moral principles. Agreeing with Kant's reasoning and adopting elements from approaches focused on the well-being of the public Sir William David Ross made some *prima facie* positions for the well-being of society summarized next[43]:

---

[41] Op. Cit, page 84.
[42] Tom Morris, *If Aristotle Ran General Motors: The New Soul of Business*, Henry Holt and Company, New York 1997, pages 146-147.
[43] Op. cit., Thiroux, page 65.

- Accuracy: Telling the truth, keeping our promises and our agreements.
- Remedy: Correcting what we have done wrong.
- Gratitude: Recognizing the good others have done for us.
- Justice: Preventing wrong-doing, grievances and proposing merit.
- Charity: Helping others to thrive, become better, and become happy.
- Self-development: helping ourselves to continually become better and be happy.
- Non-abuse: Do not harm others nor create conditions likely to cause them harm.

It is interesting that the principles formulated by Kant and Ross are very close to the principles taught in the last thirty years, in "motivational" business addresses and that principles like these existed prior to religious texts. Also, it is interesting that these are largely repetitions of past teachings of Plato, Aristotle in Nicomachean Ethics, Antigone and many others.

As we arrive in our time, moral and teleological considerations create the basis of an entrepreneurial culture, and thus the philosophical and ethical standards which define our codes of conduct. It must be reiterated that the era of societal globalization, international business and corporate governance has already imposed norms, situations and behavior that could not be predicted from the previous philosophers.

Legal versus ethical framework of reference

Perhaps at this point we should put a semicolon. Many fellow citizens would say that ethics and law are parallel frameworks. That is a convenient statement but not always true. Consider the ethical framework as a circle and the legal framework of the same societal space as another circle. These circles are positioned in an overlapping way and usually they are not of the same size.

In some cases the legal framework is ahead. It produces legislation and creates new norms that may not be associated with ethical rules. For example, some biotechnology enterprises are experimenting with genetic mutations. It is profitable[44] and very innovative scientific work. The majority of the world has not even thought about the ethical implications of a new humanoid, a mutant of a man who could be used for 'spare parts' to supply others. But the legislature, through the consultation of preselected scientific advisers, forms a clearer position which may even be different in Switzerland than in California.

In some cases the legislature intervenes to address crises, which perhaps mistakenly, were not addressed timely. Do observe that globally three different legal systems predominate: Civil law that arises from parliamentary will; code law that is judged by court-based ethical connotations; and, theocratic law, based on God-inspired beliefs. Again the culture-based dogmatic predispositions should lead our philosophical theses. Do not forget that ethics derive from philosophy and philosophy evolves on culture specificities.

Also, there are cases where the ethical framework is ahead of the legal framework. Consumers believe they have rights, but these rights are not clearly stated in the law[45]. Gradually there will be legislation. Meanwhile, advanced companies have understood the market trends and commercially cover what consumers consider as ethically necessary. Observe that corporate lobbyists may affect specificities of the legal framework, per the intentions of the companies that employ them.

But we must also consider if it is possible to have an ethical business framework in a social structure that suffers in terms of objective ethics. What happens when the government allows obvious cases, for example, of bribing, or legal violations? Moreover, is sometimes ethical for a strategically well positioned business ahead of its time to influence the way of thinking of the people and to pioneer a certain business-beneficial behavior and to impose ethical norms? Under what circumstances? Obviously, a company operating in different country environments may capitalize on relaxed moral standards to achieve questionable business objectives. And then, there are comprehensive legal frameworks that rule differently on similar cases as we are moving from one country to another... for example, the USA Foreign Corrupt Practices Act versus the

---

[44] See, for example, the cover page of the *Bloomberg Businessweek,* June 8 –June 14 2015. It writes: Rx for saving a life: 1 pill/day X 12 weeks = $94,500 How Much Should A Miracle Cost?

[45] See the consumer's rights in Chapter 4, presented for first time in 1962 by the President of the United States, John F. Kennedy.

British Antibribery Act … only very competent international lawyers can handle their approaches.

Let's put another semicolon and become iconoclastic … someone may ask … who are you to tell me what is legal for the society I live in? To a great extend *your* legal framework forces *our* ethical behavior and *our* business modus operandi. And since we are using Latin why should I respect "Pacta sunt servanda" which means "agreements must be kept"? In an era of globalization and tendency to anonymity, how do we define philosophy or ethics when within less than 24 hours I can start my brand new operation from Argentina to Belgium or from Canada to Denmark? Please, for a few minutes, follow my thinking:

Have you heard about the TOR (acronym derived from *The Onion Router*) project? The Tor Project, Inc., which started around 2012, is a Massachusetts-based 501(c)(3) research-education non-profit organization founded by computer scientists aiming to build free software for enabling anonymous communication and even to aid democracy advocates in authoritarian states. This is information technology for a new era that goes beyond the old rules of democracy that necessitated concrete legal frameworks and known individual actors[46]. To reiterate Roman law a powerful statement in the continental European legal thinking is "Nullum crimen, nulla poena sine praevia lege" which is Latin for, "There exists no crime and (therefore) no punishment without a pre-existing penal law. But who is establishing that law? Who is empowering this authority? Does this change our perception of business ethics at a time when business has become the institutional player of all societal doings? What about industries that have major impact between life and death, like military of medicine?

---

[46] A relevant ethics oriented conclusion was reached in a team effort/active learning of the undergraduate students of the University of Piraeus Giorgos Fragkos, John Rentos and Gregoria Polydera; it was stated in the following form: Many decades ago Einstein had quoted that "ethics is an exclusively human concern with no superhuman authority behind it". Nowadays the connection between internet and the lives of the people as well as the lives of the companies is both unbreakable and undeniable. So is Einstein's quote applicable to the internet today? Internet is a vast place where everyone is free to express himself however he desires, be it on a social platform like Facebook or the anonymous depths of the Deep Web. We believe that internet is neither moral nor immoral. It is what it is. It is a miniature of our society, created by the values of all the people of the globe. We are all socially responsible both for the legitimate and the illegal actions carried out there and about its morality and immorality and so it is everyone's responsibility to evolve it into something for which we will all be proud.

Welcome to our challenging new era combining globalization, legal compliance, personal philosophies, ethics and advance information technology desiderata.[47]

Succinct literature review

In this section we present a brief literature review of the academic developments regarding business ethics and revisit some of their practical dimensions that occurred during the last fifty years.

There is no doubt that economic globalization has brought many benefits to developing countries. Farhad Rassekh in his study presents research findings of scholars who analyzed and quantified the consequences of economic globalization[48]. Findings indicate that the most significant contribution of economic globalization to the Third world is the reduction of the absolute number of the very poor. In the same study it is also indicated that wellbeing is inversely correlated with poverty and economic globalization has also improved other indicators of wellbeing such as the reduction of child labor.

However in the same study it is emphasized that economic globalization is only a necessary condition, not a sufficient one, for improvement of wellbeing and economic advancement of the very poor people in developing countries for example in Asia. In the meantime on the other side of the globe in the European countries around the Mediterranean Sea some of the consequences of the global economic crisis are illustrated in the rate of increase of unemployment among young people with age less than 25 years old. Youth unemployment in some countries exceeds 50% with obvious business and ethical repercussions[49].

Furthermore, Norman Bowie in his book[50] *Business Ethics in the 21st Century* presents a critical view of business practice as it applies to ethics,

---

[47] The arguments of the three last paragraphs derived from speeches under the general title *Corporate Governance and Compliance in Health Care* that John Thanopoulos delivered at the 2015 Global MedTech Compliance Conference, May 19th 2015 and at the 11th HSSS Conference, July 10th, 2015.

[48] Rassekh, F. (2014). Economic Globalization: An Empirical Presentation and a Moral Judgment", in Business Ethics, by Michael Boylan, 2014, Second Edition, Wiley *pp* 390.

[49] Youth Unemployment in Europe. (2013) Eurostat. Retrieved from http://appsso.eurostat.ec.europa.eu/nui/submitViewTableAction.do?dvsc=8

[50] Bowie, N. E. (2013). *Business Ethics in the 21st Century*. Springer.

society, economics and strategic long term management. Bowie presents an ethically and economically supporting view of the sustainability capitalism of the European Union over the finance model of the United States. Bowie also presents a novel method for pedagogic purposes to educate students in business ethics topics. The same author in his book *Business Ethics a Kantian Perspective*, applies the principles of Kant's philosophy to the business firm in a capitalist economy[51]. He provides an insight of balanced management which is not only effective but also ethical and profitable for both stakeholders and stockholders.

Moreover, Boylan in his paper[52] examines the principle of fair competition taking into account professional, cost considerations and world interactions within modern business practice. Goodpaster and Matthews in their paper[53] examine the corporation under the prism of an individual and question whether it may have a conscience. Thomas Donaldson in his book the ethics of international business identifies a collection of critical international business rights, proposes an ethical algorithm for multinational corporations to resolve conflicts between home and host country and develops a broad, normative, framework for understanding ethics in a global market[54]. Manuel Velasquez in his book business ethics introduces concepts and cases of ethics pertaining to business, identifies business ethical issues, socio-economic conditions ensuing business ethical dilemmas, essential reasoning and analytical skills required to make ethical business decisions[55].

Kenneth Goodpaster in his paper business ethics and stakeholder analysis examines critically the relationship of ethical business decision making and stakeholder synthesis and analysis[56]. Stakeholder synthesis is categorized into multi-fiduciary yielding ethics without business and strategic yielding business without ethics. The author proposes another approach which balances ethics and management decision making through

---

[51] Bowie, N. E. (1999). *Business Ethics: A Kantian Perspective* (p. 138). Malden, MA: Blackwell Publishers.
[52] Boylan, M. (2013). The Principle of Fair Competition. Business Ethics, 155.
[53] Goodpaster, K. E., & Matthews JR, J. B. (2013). A. The Corporation as an Individual Can a Corporation Have a Conscience?. Business Ethics, 55.
[54] Donaldson, T. (1989). The ethics of international business (p. 7). New York: Oxford University Press.
[55] Velasquez, M. G., & Velazquez, M. (2002). Business ethics: Concepts and cases (5th ed., p. 528). Upper Saddle River, NJ: Prentice Hall.
[56] Goodpaster, K. E. (1991). Business ethics and stakeholder analysis. Business Ethics Quarterly, 53-73.

new stakeholder thinking avoiding the ethics or business paradox and clarifying for managers and board of directors ethical considerations in business decision making.

Donaldson and Dunfee in their article[57] propose a new unified theory of business ethics which categorizes ethical obligations based upon two levels of consent. The first level is the theoretical "macrosocial" contract appealing to all rational contractors and the second level is the real, empirical "microsocial" contract agreed by members of many localized communities. This approach attempts to provide a framework for unification of normative and empirical business ethics research methods.

Andrew Stark in his article[58] recognizes the conflict between business interests and ethics and acknowledges that the real business world is not black and white but is entangled with a variety of mixed motives. He describes business decision makers as managers who have mixed motives and are not always purely altruistic or self-interested and are assigned difficult business ethical dilemmas which they have to resolve using moderation, pragmatism and minimalism.

Joseph Weiss in his book[59] categorizes internal and external stakeholders and examines their interrelationship with self-interests, business interests, moral leadership, corporate values, self-regulation, decision making and ethical dilemmas in a global market environment. Richard De George in his book[60] describes ethics as the cohesive substance required for successful business enterprises. He describes how concepts of business ethics influence and affect management, production, marketing, finance, workers' rights, environmental issues and business decision making.

Andrew Crane and Dirk Matten in their book[61] describe how business ethics affect corporate social responsibility, corporate citizenship, globalization and sustainability. They focus on business ethics from the European management perspective. They describe European business

---

[57] Donaldson, T., & Dunfee, T. W. (1994). Toward a unified conception of business ethics: Integrative social contracts theory. Academy of management review, 19(2), 252-284.

[58] Stark, A. (1993). What's the matter with business ethics?. Harvard business review, 71(3), 38.

[59] Weiss, J. W. (2008). Business ethics: a stakeholder and issues management approach.

[60] De George, R. T. (2009). Business ethics. Pearson Education.

[61] Crane, A., & Matten, D. (2007). Business ethics: Managing corporate citizenship and sustainability in the age of globalization. Oxford University Press.

ethics and how they interrelate to multinational and international business ethics. Elizabeth Creyer in her article[62] examines the influences of business ethics on consumer purchase intention and finds that corporate ethical behavior will influence positively consumers and unethical corporate behavior will influence negatively consumer purchasing decisions.

Moreover, Donaldson and Dunfee in their book[63] give a perspective of business ethics from the point of view of a social contract. They acknowledge that international businesses influence government policy and to ensure ethical business behavior they propose a social contract between the international business and the people they interact. This social contract takes into consideration human rights, public sentiment and local cultures. Hoffman Frederick and Schwartz in their book examine corporate conscience, reverse discrimination, ethical management and managed care coexistence[64].

Reidenbach and Robin in their paper propose an improvement in the ethics scales inventory published in a 1988 Journal of Business Ethics article. They describe the distillation and validation process whereby the original thirty-three item inventory is reduced to eight items which comprise the ethical dimensions of moral equity, relativism and contractualism. The multidimensional ethics scale demonstrates significant predictive ability[65]. Beltramini Peterson and Kozmetsky in their paper study the consideration of business ethics by young college students who are the future business leaders. Their findings indicate that females are more concerned with business ethics than males and college students in general show an increased interest, awareness and concern about business ethics.[66] Beauchamp, Bowie and Arnold in their book examine ethical theory and

[62] Creyer, E. H. (1997). The influence of firm behavior on purchase intention: do consumers really care about business ethics?. Journal of consumer Marketing, 14(6), 421-432.
[63] Donaldson, T., & Dunfee, T. W. (1999). Ties that bind: A social contracts approach to business ethics. Harvard Business Press.
[64] Hoffman, W. M., Frederick, R. E., Schwartz M. S. (2000). Business ethics: Readings and cases in corporate morality. New York: McGraw-Hill.
[65] Reidenbach, R. E., & Robin, D. P. (1990). Toward the development of a multidimensional scale for improving evaluations of business ethics. Journal of Business Ethics, 9(8), 639-653.
[66] Beltramini, R. F., Peterson, R. A., & Kozmetsky, G. (1984). Concerns of college students regarding business ethics. Journal of Business Ethics, 3(3), 195-200. Fiat's ad, pages 114-115.

business practice, the purpose of the corporation, the ethical treatment of employees, marketing and disclosure of information, ethical issues in information technology, corporate character and individual responsibility, acceptable risk, diversity and discrimination in the workplace and ethical issues in international business.[67]

Aspects from philosophy of information technology[68], [69]

One big question frequently asked is whether information technology can cover all real needs of humanity. Many advances have been made towards this direction during the last decades, but the opinions diverge. Information systems studies operate for too long but with too little philosophical underpinning.

Over the last 50 years the IT competition has been transformed two times. During the 1st period, in the 60's, individual activities in the value chain have been automated such as bill paying, resource planning and computer

---

[67] Beauchamp, T. L., Bowie, N. E., & Arnold, D. G. (Eds.). (2004). Ethical theory and business.

[68] Philosophy of Information may be defined as the philosophical field concerned with (a) the critical investigation of the conceptual nature and basic principles of information, including its dynamics, utilization, and sciences, and (b) the elaboration and application of information-theoretic and computational methodologies to philosophical problems, according to Floridi (2004).

[69] This subchapter was contributed by the Doctoral student at the University of Piraeus, Nikos Papazoglou. He is using as the following references:

- Floridi, Luciano, The information society and its philosophy: Introduction to the special issue on "The philosophy of information, its nature, and future developments, The information society, Volume 25, 2009, pages 153–158.
- Floridi, Luciano, The fourth revolution: How the infosphere is reshaping human reality. Oxford University. 2014.
- Floridi, Luciano, Open problems in the philosophy of information, Metaphilosophy, Volume 35, Number 4, 2004, pages 554–582.
- Floridi, Luciano, What is the philosophy of information? Metaphilosophy, Volume 33, Number 1 & 2, 2002, pages 123–145.
- Henderson, Hazel, Philosophical conflict: Reexamining the goals of knowledge, Public Administration Review, Volume 35, Number 1, 1975, pages 77-80.
- Stahl, Bernd Carsten, Morality, ethics, and reflection: A categorization of normative information systems research, Journal of the association for Information systems, Volume 13, Issue 8, August 2012, pages 636-656.
- Willcocks, Leslie and Whitley, Edgar A., Developing the information and knowledge agenda in information systems: insights from philosophy, The Information Society, Volume 25, 2009, pages 190–197.
- Yip, Elijah and Hsia, Martin E., Confidentiality in the Cloud: The Ethics of Using Cloud Services in the Practice of Law, The Computer & Internet Lawyer, Volume 31, Number 12, 2014, pages 19-25.

design. The 2nd wave on IT competition began in the 80's with the rise of the inexpensive Internet and the connectivity.

Now we are in the brink of the 3rd wave with key characteristic the improvement of the product itself. More particularly, computers are being put inside the products and are connected to the internet and among them. This cloud data is stored and analyzed to improve product functionality and performance. The 3rd wave has the potential to be the most hopeful and improve economic growth more than the previous two waves.

However, processing such a huge amount of information is challenging and only people owning deep knowledge of information analysis can handle so enormous amount of data. Thus, we conclude again that only people possessing the technology can set the new rules. Such aspects of Information Technology are affected by the corporate or the industry they refer to and the place they are established. Also, philosophy of technology refers to the self-awareness of a society and its normativity[70].

Hence, there is conflict of interests between the corporate's and the society's benefits. Firms produce (potentially) unethical products or services which contradict the social and environmental interest. For example, the oil and gas industry has caused monstrous damage to the air and the seas. Medicines have to be tested to experimental animals and human in order to be finally produced and biotechnology can lead to a new generation of people with specific characteristics. The military industry produces weapons of mass destruction and the nuclear power can be used to make even more powerful weapons. In contrast to the above, our life has been advanced due to these products. Even the Research and Development in the military industry has helped to improve our lives such as the creation of the personal computers or the artificial parts of the human bodies.

Apart from the above mentioned the significant expectation of personal privacy is vital in a society which becomes more and more online. Sensitive personal data are uploaded unceasingly in the info-sphere[71] and nobody knows who can have access to them. Hackers can intercept calls,

---

[70] Normativity is a term used by Bernd Carsten Stahl to classify words with similar meaning like ethics and morality.

[71] Information and Communication Technologies (ICTs) constitute the infosphere. A commonly known word created by Floridi referring to the environment in which we live.

messages, photographs, bank accounts, passwords and any kind of online information. Cloud computing does not guarantee security and privacy of the personal details. Big Data can offer solutions to various aspects of our life, but at the same time it can destroy humanity. The one-way solution to the probable risk of Big Data is to find the strict framework in which all data will be secure even though for the time being this seems impossible.

Humanity is in the onset of a mutation, the outcome of which is questionable. Perhaps, a few charismatic and perspicacious authors have already given a taste of the future. George Orwell (*1984*, written in 1948) believed that one day there will be thought control. Big Data can gather all our moves and (why not) thoughts. Additionally, firms have already enshrined copyrights for televisions with integrated camera and microphone. Aldus Huxley (*Brave New World*, 1932) wrote that the media will educate people to consume. Finally, H. G. Wells (*A Modern Utopia*, 1905) claimed that in the future there will be just a powerful and rich group of people which will govern the world.

Harsh criticism is made towards information technology and its influence in everyday life. Feenberg believes that scientific-technical rationality has become a new culture and that critical thinking is needed to apply institutions to control the actions of those possessing the technology and not the technology itself. However, people should not be absolute or naïve with technology and support hypocritically that "Guns don't kill people, people kill people". There is a wide number of products that verifies it.

Implanted chips below the skin can connect wirelessly to a devise and inform people about their health. Since they are healthy they will be able to find a job. This same microchip is able to pay and keep the unique personal details, like an electronic footprint of each one's life. "Smart systems" will be able to know people's habits and their will to do something before they need it and they will be wirelessly connected to their desired devices.

> "This recognition produces paranoia on all sides, as new priesthoods threaten old ones clinging to the thrones of the domain of science policy. Where the ends of knowledge are power, science becomes the servant of the powerful." Hazel Henderson[72]

---

[72] Henderson, Hazel, Philosophical conflict: Reexamining the goals of knowledge, Public Administration Review, Volume 35, Number 1, 1975, pages 77-80.

Business ethics issues revisited

Adding to the discussion of the previous section and starting from the developed world countries, we may observe that today the concepts of corporate governance and finance are interrelated and depend directly on business ethics. The leaders of the business are the members of the respective Board of Directors representing the shareholders-financiers with a key role to recruit, monitor and, if necessary, replace the head manager of the company. Indeed, in more sophisticated models of business management[73], the Board's role focuses on creating leaders who can make effective decisions as to reverse inefficient policies.

Pioneering the business ethics concept, back in 1974, Max Ways wrote in *Fortune Magazine* a very revealing of the new era of business ethics article entitled "Business faces growing pressures to behave better". In the same issue there is an advertisement from Fiat, pointing to its very minute vehicle by the then standards, stressing that the "yesterday's symbol of status is today's symbol of excess"[74]. Since then, less than half a century ago, many business concepts in terms of philosophy and ethics have changed dramatically.

Certainly the funding of an organization is not limited to the contributions of the shareholders. The business plan determines the risks and levels of bank debt as well as the contribution of all stakeholders who may have their own opinion on business ethics. Further, it is necessary for the reader to understand that, at the macro-economic level, the global financial downturns are directly linked to business (un)ethics of the heads of financial institutions who may have been elected to avoid implementing strict banking criteria.

Another critical issue is the origin of the members of the Board and the managers who may influence business ethics policy and business operations[75]. In addition, the reader has to observe that legally

---

[73] Pound, J. (1995). The promise of the governed corporation. *Harvard Business Review*, 73(2), 89-98.

[74] *Fortune Magazine,* May 1974, pages 193-195 and 310, 314, 316, 319-320.

[75] For example a study of internationalization of corporate Boards of Nordic firms finds that although they have a small percentage of international foreign-origin directors they are related to financial internationalization rather than foreign sales, and thus to the monitoring rather than advisory functions which are also served by national directors.Oxelheim, L., Gregorič, A., Randøy, T., & Thomsen, S. (2013). On the internationalization of corporate boards: The case of Nordic firms. Journal of International Business Studies, 44(3), 173-194.

shareholders are owners of the business but they have no legal or financial responsibility for the activities of their firm and they have limited information or ability to take corporate decisions[76]. It is also interesting to examine how cross-cultural influences affect the ethical operations of our global village. For example, whereas Chinese directors of financial institutions may use eastern philosophy to guide their business ethics decisions, Europeans may have more Christian-based tendencies[77].

Using Max Ways concept, business realization of the need to *behave better* effectively starts at the beginning of new millennium--at least for the developed world and the larger corporate entities. Moreover, the scandal of Enron, has brought to the attention of the public formal cases of mismanagement of large enterprises. Irrespective if the root cause of losses may have been intentional or not, all these cases indicated problems at the highest level of corporate management[78]. It is interesting that today, world-wide, a new generation of managers and country leaders, having being taught philosophy and business ethics, are taking charge and remodel the societal fabric[79]. Though it has been said that "*However wise it may be to glean wisdom from the past, it is folly to regard the past as the*

---

[76] Anand, S. (2007). Essentials of corporate governance (Vol. 36). Wiley.

[77] In China often giving loans depends on Confucius philosophy of the relationship of the loan receiver to the patriarchic family structure as it is a good predictor of paying back the loan.Dexter Roberts (2012). Confucius Makes a Comeback in China, *Bloomberg Businessweek* 11 November.

[78] John A. Byrne, et al., (2002) How to Fix Corporate Governance, BusinessWeek, May 6, 2002, pages 44-45. Here are some examples of that era:
January 10 2000, America on Line (AOL) buys Time Warner for $183 billion. Within just two years the purchase is proven questionable at a value of $54 billion.
March 10 2000, the high-tech stock exchange index, NASDAQ, is at 5048. 30 months later is below 1800.
January 2001, the general manager of Oracle, selling off part of its shares to an impressive personal gain of $706 million. Some weeks later the earnings forecasts of Oracle are lowered.
February 2001, Arthur Levitt Jr., departs his position as head of the U.S. Securities and Exchange Commission SEC, when the business lobby discovers his plan to ban audit firms to be business advisers for the companies they audit.
May 2001, Arthur Andersen agreed to pay $110,000,000 to shareholders of Sunbeam for questionable practices in the auditing of the company.
December 2, 2001, Enron declares bankruptcy.
January 22 2002, Credit Suisse First Boston agrees to pay $100 million in fines on charges of systematically questionable practices for trading shares.
April 1 2001, Xerox agrees to pay a SEC fine of $10 million on charges of dubious accounting practices.

[79] Observe the "under age 50" group in terms of country and corporate leadership.

exclusive source of truth. Truth is relative and expanding; it lives always in the present, achieving new expression in each generation of men--even in each human life ",[80] expect that changes cannot come abruptly. People in power have vested interests and may react.

---

[80] *The Urantia Book*, Urantia Foundation, Chicago, Illinois 1955, page 888.

CHAPTER 2

THE SOCIETY OF THE 21ST CENTURY

What you will learn in this Chapter

In this chapter you will learn ...
- That socio-cultural elements that have characterized previous times, during the last decades are changing.
- That the needs of modern times may require us to see under different light the philosophical and moral lessons we inherited from our ancestors.
- That between cultures and economic systems there are significant differences of understanding and principles.
- That the electronic age and mass media established the elements of knowledge and information in everyday life.
- About cultural and economic information from different places as well as mutations in the global institutional framework.
- Evidence of contemporary global realities, such as transational organizations, intergovernmental agreements, economic conflicts, security, and so on.
- The existence and the reasons for strong contrasts between 'haves' and 'have nots'.

Introduction to Chapter 2

The previous chapter presented philosophy and ethics concepts, primarily of Western-type societies, as developed in the last 3,000 years. In this chapter we discuss about the realities of our time and how they change the way of thinking and behavior of the modern man. This chapter adds to the theory of ethics the rapidly changing realities of 21st century and links it to Chapter 3 which deals with the needs of the new societal institution, the global business.

During the last two hundred years we experienced technological changes that totally redefined quality of life, creation of new institutions, social priorities, meaning of work, welfare dependency, family structure, media influences, individualism, application of inventions, social equality, freedom of the individual, global citizenship and so on. During the last two hundred years the industrial revolution brought into our lives the engine, the airplane, the computer, information technologies, genetic mutations, or the ability to conquest close-by stars. During the last two hundred years we have removed most barriers to the movement of people, capital and technology, formulated principles such as "equal rights", we have direct communication and control in almost every corner of the globe, we have introduced new ways of thinking, social being, fighting each other, living together and new philosophical concepts.

While we continue to rely on the data and predispositions of the past, we are facing challenges that require agile reaction and detailed knowledge. Nowadays, the capacity of information devices doubles in less than two years, and information proliferates at a similarly fast rate creating strong personal renewal requirements, competition work, questions of data quality and , therefore, of social adjustment. This phenomenon is clearly more pronounced in developed societies where the basis of coexistence with others, perhaps because their priorities have changed should be revised[81]. Let alone that the human enterprise is able to move in accordance to demand and even in a virtual way[82].

Transnational, social and cultural thought differences

Previously, we mentioned that the topography defines the socio-cultural dimension of the people who settled there, and by extension, the corresponding philosophy and ethics. Tropical forests, vast deserts, high mountains and seas formed the first human borders of nature and within these environments populations evolved. Over the years people have created the foundations of culture, depending on the elements of nature

---

[81] Take, for example statistics of marriages and divorces in the United States as a percentage of 1,000 residents. In 1998, there were 8.8 marriages in 1000 residents and there were 4.2 divorces. The corresponding statistics for 1920 were 12 marriages per 1,000 inhabitants and down to 1.9 divorces. Source: *(The) World Almanac and Book of Facts 2000*, Primedia Reference Inc., World Almanac Books, Mahwah, New Jersey 1999, page 889.

[82] We shall address the topic at the next chapter. However, here are some useful references that in our opinion helped to reshape the understanding of the topic: Davidow, William H. & Michael S. Malone, *The Virtual Corporation: Restructuring and Revitalizing the Corporation for the 21st Century*, Harper Business, New York 1993; Hammer, Michael and James Champy, *Reengineering the Corporation: A Manifesto for Business Revolution*, Harper Business, New York 1993; Pasternack, Bruce A., and Albert J. Viscio, *The Centerless Corporation: A New Model for Transforming your Organization for Growth and Prosperity*, Simon and Schuster, New York, 1998.

and environmental living conditions they had to face. For example, the needs of the people who settled at the Mediterranean basin, with a temperate climate and fruitful earth, were quite different from the needs of people who reached and settled in Scandinavia or the Sahara.

The manners and customs, reflecting the topographical features, gradually evolved into complex legal, financial, bureaucratic systems. With their armies and their armada-imposed precise boundaries were no longer mountains or deserts that divided the people. Languages and religions created even further variations. During periods of peace cultural and commercial exchanges took place. During periods of war international borders re-allocation took place. People built very high walls to keep themselves protected within the walls and this artificial security ensured that their cultures continued to be diversified from those of the invaders.

Perhaps it is symbolic of an upcoming change in 1883 ... the Statue of Liberty, a gift from France to America which was erected on an island in front of New York for the thousands of immigrants to see arriving in the country with so many opportunities, yet it was built somewhere in the area of des Champs-Elysées in Paris. "Freedom illuminates the world" was the name given to it by the sculptor, emphasizing characteristic trends of the time, as democracy for all, equal rights, rule of law, free speech[83].

Travel and knowledge transfer was very difficult before the discovery of the steamship and the telegraph. The steamship and the telegraph were break-through technological inventions which revolutionized human life and the way of thinking. Their introduction to the lives of people has changed their daily routine, their institutions, their principles and their ethics.

It's about half a century that the airplane was able to reach supersonic speeds and little more than a quarter of a century that the internet came into our lives. With better communication among people we were able to achieve much more than our predecessors. The possibility of communication, the virtual absence of barriers for all people of our time, the globalized media and many other innovations, suddenly made it possible to show the disparity among economic classes of people and may

---

[83] Christopher Dickey, Fears in the 'Un-America', *Newsweek*, 11 February 2002, page 10.

give rise to conflicts between the people who 'haves' and the people who 'have not' or the emergence of cultural conflicts.

In a parallel sense, we can see that while countries (still) play a key role in the events of the world community, the big international corporations continuously acquire a more substantial presence in the world progress and social development. Let us not forget that large international corporations have turnover well above the GDP of most individual states or individual countries. Therefore, it is not beyond conceivable thought that large commercial business interests indirectly retain regulatory capacity to influence, create, alter and maintain interstate and international laws and agreements.

Introducing the 21st century: A new very sensitive world

It is clear that in a world of information very easily one can hear the suffering in a distant part of the world, the opportunities offered there, the need to stand by the less fortunate in order to reduce the startling differences between poor and wealthy. These differences from one point of view could be opposite poles causing ruptures and from another perspective they can be causes for productivity and progress.

Let us, hypothesize that we really want to help. The road to hell, they say that it is paved with good intentions. For example, the more economically developed part of a united Europe now gives, with presumably good intentions, financial assistance to developing regions in order to thrive and advance their economic status. However, is it so easy for a farmer somewhere in rural Italy, or for a fisherman, somewhere in a remote Greek island, to be properly informed and, within a set time to complete a complex application and prepare the 14 prerequisite-documents and certificates, while in all his life he has been able to obtain only a few public documents, such as the graduation certificate from the elementary school, the birth certificate of his child or a driver's license? Perhaps we are facing a complex social bureaucracy that does not allow the uneducated man to savor the benefits from an advanced societal structure.

The people of the example might be worthy and creative. Perhaps though they may feel marginalized, weak and prisoners of a way of thinking and a bureaucratic practice they do not understand. Perhaps they may be prone to reactions. Think now, not of the undereducated Italian farmers and Portuguese fishermen, but think of the really poor in a native forest in

Brazil or the Kalahari Desert. How they can come into the 21st century? And yet, let us consider the revolutionary young person in Afghanistan, Pakistan, Colombia, Nicaragua and Palestine who acquired a stimulus from the new global communications media and prepared a response and the elders of the tribe lead him to react in favor of a certain social or religious cause.

With journalistic interest, but basically with a social apathy, the developed world for over twenty years is observing the existence of individual antithetical poles causing intense reaction. From the skinheads in Germany, to the group 17 November in Greece, the group which released gas in the Japanese subway and the bombers of the Federal building in Oklahoma, there was one common denominator: Violent reactions to the established accepted social systems, which largely could have been avoided and prevented if the necessary measures had been taken in advance of the catastrophes.

Half a century ago, in the classic book La Galaxie Gutenberg face à l' ère électronique, Marshall M. McLuhan speaks of social transformation from the human in a group to the society of people. It is an era of progressive and linear consciousness, a direct product of technological evolution and dynamics that such a development ensues. It is reasonable, then, if we accept the position of McLuhan, like so many other philosophers and communicators, we are to face a time when philosophical and ethical trends, which evolved in millennia, can change dramatically following the requirements of our technological age.

Moreover, and although that statistics indicate that a significant portion of the world's inhabitants do not use the phone or make regular use of internet, the intensification of the messages from the media give great masses of people, from Italy to Indonesia and from Canada to China, new symbols, new incentives and new values. Within a few years, mass media enabled people to learn of events in distant countries. People learned about other lifestyles, religions, technologies, cultures. Everyone saw the facility that could create new wealth, power, and glory. Everyone saw the convenience that could bypass disciplined priorities of the past to borrow money to buy happiness. The individual noted that science fiction books of the past were right giving prophecies of individual-centered societies. And often the individual was "confused". The principles that the person had learned might not go very well in the information age. The collision of north-south, of rich and poor, of entire cultures, was *ante portas*.

The tragic memories of the aircraft which fell on September 11, 2001 in the dual towers of New York, the Pentagon and in Pennsylvania were another sign of a new era which had already arrived, but remained incomprehensible. After two world wars in the past century, the peace work of the League of Nations and the United Nations, the great achievements of the era of globalization and international associations that offered so much security, the world was again faced with uncertainty, anxiety and doubt. What was meant to happen in this new era?[84] But let's see how modern journalism sees some of the main themes of today[85]:

Farewell to isolationism

From Rome and Byzantium to China, and more recently, from England and France to the USA postwar superpowers and Russia, the people have created "divisions" between them, somehow defining defenses against foreign invaders who spoke other languages and have other customs and traditions. Within their area people have developed their own lifestyles and behavior and their philosophical underpinnings and morality. The needs of international trade, learning, and progress teach us tolerance, methodology and adaptation of human behavior and virtually eliminate the need of the isolationist country-state.

In all history of civilizations national independence was based on the creation of barriers, military, social, economic. In an age of globalization, mass media and technology, this is no longer desirable at the national levels. Bringing down country frontiers and allowing intermixing of populations has created a new global status quo. Moreover, the immediacy of information creates learning stimuli, new challenges, rivalry, adaptation and imitation.

Opening up national borders is also very challenging especially during an economic crisis. For example in Europe where the national borders are open for the citizens of European Union member states there are critics against this open border policy, the Euro skeptics. The challenge here is to overcome skepticism with a growing economy for all Europeans to benefit.

---

[84] John Rossant, A Fragile World, *BusinessWeek*, February 11, 2002, page 24.
[85] Some ideas were taken from the special edition for Davos of the magazine *Newsweek*, December 2001-February 2002, the general topic Issues 2002.

Cultural conflicts

It is this elimination of barriers, which gives rise to conflict at another level. It is not possible for generations that followed, for example, a religious trend suddenly and comfortably to accept the existence of another religion and accept the new ways and the new faith. For years political leaders spoke of the "evil demon" or "Red Bear". Tens of millions of people believed and died defending those beliefs which now many refer to as simplifications of an earlier era. At the beginning of this chapter we talked about international sociocultural differences of thought and, on this topic the cause for possible conflicts between the people who 'have' and the people who 'have not' or the emergence of cultural conflict. The latter is no longer in the field of probability. It is real, it takes modern cultural and business forms, and imposes new models of balancing tendencies.

There can be no denial of our cultural past, because this oblivion betrays us. People identify with groups defined in terms of culture: tribes, ethnic groups, religious communities, nations, and in a wider sense, civilizations[86]. In a world that is now virtually without borders, the following position of Professor Huntington is important: The people seeking identity and rediscovering their nationality, need enemies. The potentially most dangerous hostility is developed along the 'border line' between the major cultures of the world[87]. Friction between cultures is possible for many reasons such as promotion of a culture, missionary policy, expansionary policy, general political, business aspirations, etc. In this reasoning, we must add that businesses listed on various stock exchanges can electronically transfer their profits at Swiss banks and from there to the route for training and purchasing equipment of a private military unit in Montana USA for a Muslim group, or a social response unit in Afghanistan.

But we must realize that there are cultural conflicts within the same country, based on culture, color, sex, age, social or economic class. Only very recently, there is a consciousness awareness of class and racial issues. One of the most classic photos of 1976, shows a white student in Boston USA holding as a spear the pole of an American flag, trying to pin an

---

[86] Samuel P. Huntington, *The Clash of Civilizations and the reshuffling of World Order*, Third Edition, Terzo Books, Athens 2001, pages 23-24.
[87] Ibid., page 21. For example, "the 48 ethnic conflicts that have occurred worldwide in 1993, almost half were between groups belonging to different cultures", ibid., page 44.

African American shouting "get the ni**er!"[88] This is an extreme example against the law and while laws tend to limit the existence of such differences, there are still causes of internal social frictions.

At the same time, and given our tendency for cross-border alliance formation and the relatively unclear understanding of cultural context, the business language becomes of paramount importance, similar to state colonization of past eras where the language was the defining instrument of successful ruling. Unquestionably, successful business dealings today require respect of local languages, but one should consider the conceptual overtones that are teachable at the headquarters, thousands of miles away[89]. Consider also the opposite, for example English becoming the universal option of choice at least for finance reporting[90]!

Global security

For many years Russia, which still today possesses an impressive military force, tried in vain and despite the significant human and material losses, to prevail in Afghanistan. Some years later, the USA, after the events of September 11, based on a highly organized military effort, managed to prevail in Afghanistan. Geographically ranging thousands of miles beyond Russia, the USA military realized its aim quickly and with minimum casualties.

Entering the 21st century the well lubricated military machines are highly efficient with laser focus and rapid surgical intervention. Theoretically, at least in the developed Western world, the existing military capacity has the ability to adequately protect the business interests of their citizens, in

[88] See tribute magazine *Life*, December 1979, Special issue, The 70s: The Decade in Pictures, page 180.

[89] Amol M Joshi and Nandini Lahiri, Language friction and partner selection in cross-border R&D alliance formation, *Journal of International Business Studies,* Volume 46, Issue 2 (February/ March 2015), pages 123-152. Also, W Travis Selmier II, Aloysius Newenham-Kahindi and Chang Hoon Oh, "Understanding the words of relationships": Language as an essential tool to manage CSR in communities of place, *Journal of International Business Studies,* Volume 46, Issue 2 (February/ March 2015), pages 153-179.

[90] Thomas Jeanjean, Hervé Stolowy, Michael Erkens and Teri Lombardi Yohn, International evidence on the impact of adopting English as an external reporting language, *Journal of International Business Studies,* Volume 46, Issue 2 (February/ March 2015), pages 180-205.

the same way that earlier the financial interests of the colonies were protected by the war machinery of the mother country. There is certainly different quality of military machines and traditional military art has evolved dramatically. The question is: Do we any longer need these military enforcement mechanisms where the lack of barriers and globalization specify new types of business attack and enforcement? Should there also be new approaches that can manage the challenges of globalization and ever-changing authorities, perhaps through new economic agreements that require control while facing non-conventional conflicts and will provide the guarantees of free movement of goods and frictionless world trade?[91]

For example, Naomi Klein writes that rather than face the challenge set by the attacks of September 11 2001 creating the appropriate security infrastructure, the US government discovered a new role for this: the supply of security expertise from the market. So, just two months after the fall of the Twin Towers in New York, the US Department of Defense has brought groups of specialist consultants with experience in high technology sectors to help in the war on terrorism, implicitly accepting the inadequacy of past approaches[92].

Further, in observing the complexity of today's world could anyone have doubts about whether the current think tanks and intellectuals actually have the opportunity to study and develop new models of modern principles and objectives? Wolfe says that "intellectuals who responded to the Vietnam War, supported the positions of the universal principles such as human rights and world peace. Today's revolutionaries have a limited understanding of the world"[93]. Do we find ourselves in an era in which traditional military tactics have very limited value and, for example, instead of the country states, military must protect businesses?

---

[91] Fareed Zakaria, A plan for global security, *Newsweek*, December 2001-February 2002, special issue on "Issues 2002", pages 16-17.

[92]Naomi Klein, *The Shock Doctrine: The Rise of Disaster Capitalism*, Allen Lane-Penguin Books, London 2007, pages 199-300, literally, the Department of Defense brought together what it described as "a small group of venture capitalist consultants" with experience in the dot-com sector.

[93] "Intellectuals who opposed the Vietnam War appealed to universal values like human rights and world peace. Today's reactionaries offer a crabbed and confined view of the world" Alan Wolfe, It's all our fault, *Newsweek*, December 2001-February 2002, special issue on "Issues 2002", page 48.

Economic and financial conflicts

An alien from another planet will be surprised to see the disparities of wealth and means on Earth. For example maybe one-fifth of the global citizens are coming from the so called developed countries; still they represent more than fifty per cent of the global purchasing power. Then there is this huge area, Africa, where its inhabitants control less than five percent of the global buying power but they represent more than ten percent of the planet's population. Therefore, comparing purchasing power and population masses, this alien will note that there are serious differences between people who "have" and people who "have-not". However, the same applies within countries. In general few people have lots of money whereas the masses are at opposite side of the spectrum.

Following the same thinking, and given the global economic crisis of 2008-2015, in his extreme naïveté someone may ask … what is the difference between a shark that eats you alive and a banker that threatens you to get everything you have if you have not paid all that is due to him? Why is the difference between the super-rich who travels in his private jet from one of his estates to another while thousands of kids die of hunger in poverty stricken parts of the world? Whom does the law protect when if someone steals in order to feed his family is doing something wrong whereas the ruler of the country has no problem to marry eighty wives?

Back to the global economic crisis of 2008-2015: At that time the discussions in Wall Street, Washington DC and Brussels were centered in the world economy. International business and political leaders of the largest corporate and national economies of the globe were facing one of the most formidable crises in the recent world economic history. Although the housing market drop was one of the most significant in the recent US economic history, signs of trouble were visible years earlier starting with the hi-tech market demise. Examining the reasoning of this international economic crisis one identifies a poly-parametric problem. Experts agree that the complex financial instruments that derivatives specialists and finance experts created to take advantage of high risk investments to maximize profits led to the optimum conditions for a chain reaction starting with the US housing market demise which then led to the international stock markets ensuing decay which then led to the decline of many national economies around the world. To put it in plain terms knowledge deficit and profit seeking speculators planted the seeds of a wooden giant weak at the roots who easily bowed to the ground at the first sign of a strong storm.

The trends, however, indicate a reversal of this situation. By some, by 2050 countries like Brazil, Russia, India or China, presently being developing economies, will control about the two-thirds of the worlds' Gross National Product. Meanwhile, the planet needs to be reconsidering its financial, banking, credit and debt situation for it promotes inequalities and supports a system of social injustice.

More contradictions and hyper-capitalism

Indeed, the world is much easier to travel, especially for those of us who are in the developed countries. Still there are many obstacles requiring very careful movements. Previously we discussed our very fragile world and the dimensions that highlight this fragility. Beyond cultural and economic conflicts that require maintenance of military systems and development of transnational treaties and accords, there are other reasons, perhaps more tangible and largely associated with the overall evolution of a republic, highlighting the contrasts between countries and the distance between the people who "have" and the people who "have not". The contradictions can be causes of conflict and may destroy the delicate balance which now exists.

Population growth: For example, let us take the predicted increase (or decrease) of population of some countries. In some countries populations are growing remarkably quickly. Worldwide, Uganda and Niger are expected to have great population growth. At the other extreme are Ukraine and Georgia losing in the immediate predictable future more than one-third of their population.

Births: In countries like Angola, Niger and Uganda it is common to have about fifty babies per 1,000 people born in a year, whereas countries such as Austria, Bulgaria, Germany, Japan or Russia, the ratio is less than 10 babies in 1,000 people. Observe also that in 2013 the average number of children born to a woman in:

- Africa were 4.7, from 6.7 in 1970.
- Asia were 2.2, from 5.4 in 1970.
- Europe were 1.6, from 2.3 in 1970.
- Latin America & Caribbean were 2.2, from 5.3 in 1970.
- North America were 1.8, from 2.3 in 1970.[94]

We conclude, therefore, that in the 21st century the population growth will steadily declining, as compared with only fifty years ago.

Age of population: As the population median age we define the number where we have equal numbers of people above and below it. At one extreme, there are countries like Uganda and Niger with median age less than twenty years of age. At the other extreme, with a population median more than forty we have we have countries like Japan and Italy. Obviously, population youth creates social inferences for work force potential, as well as for overall experience and philosophical maturity.

Urbanization: Already more than half of the world's population lives in cities. In contrast, less than 20% of population lives in cities in countries such as Uganda, Nepal and Ethiopia. It is expected that the trend of urbanization creates new social living and individual priorities[95].

Standard of living: Measured in per capita GDP brings countries like Luxembourg, Bermuda and Norway are at the top whereas countries such as Burundi, Ethiopia or Congo are at the other extreme, with average income several hundred times less. Measured by the human development index, an index that combines adult literacy and life expectancy, we find at the top positions countries like Canada, Japan, USA or Scandinavia, whereas at the other side of the spectrum we find Niger, Sierra Leone and Chad.

---

[94] Carl Haub and Toshiko Kaneda, 2014 World Population Data Sheet, Washington DC, Population Reference Bureau, 2014.
[95] See a special issue of the *American Scientist* (Better Cities) September 2011, pages 62-75.

<u>Economic growth:</u> In an era where an economic crisis is focused on financial indicators, average GDP growth is of paramount importance. Again, presently major developing nations are leading the growth spectrum, whereas some of the developed countries are forced to reexamine their debt structures in order to maintain and not depress their economic preeminence. In tandem with the economic growth issue are other measures of national economic activity, like inflation, exchange rates and overall reserves.

From the above consider ...
- Economic reasons for population migration.
- Where immigrants are needed and where do they come from, taking into account size and compatibility of 'culture' or education?
- The so-called phenomenon of magnetism or magnet effect, where by millions of people are attracted to Europe and North America[96].
- Why there is such a huge difference in some statistics, such as population density or abortion.
- What impact the economic development of a country may have to expand the future map of the global village.
- What impact the inflation, amount of borrowing, credit, interest and foreign trade may have in stability and the development of an economy?
- External assistance that a country receives. Industrial and rural infrastructure and related development variables. Existence of minerals, underground resources, strategic materials and energy.

Previously we wrote that reported contradictions like these can be causes of conflict and destroy the delicate balance that now exists between countries. Still we must realize that only in the last 100 years people were able to record reliably comparative statistics. In addition only during the past 50 years there has been substantial communication and analysis of these data.

It should be added that we are facing a reversal of economic data in the worldwide level. Countries that were considered "developing", forty years ago, will far surpass the GDP of present 'developed' countries. It is expected that with their economic progress these neo-plutocratic countries

---

[96] A tale of two bellies, *The Economist*, August 24, 2002, page 11, and in the same issue, Special Report: Demography and the West, pages 20-22.

will impose their own philosophical and ethical codes that were buried for centuries according to the alleged inferiority of these colonized or underdeveloped countries. Therefore, substantial knowledge of financial and cultural differences between people creates new challenges and new ethical priorities, because of the modern technological reality and the impact of media which can lead to mutations of institutions.

We present the reader, with an example from modern American economy, of the previous proposal for mutation of institutions: It is true that prosperity that has grown over the last ten years is a stable sign of progress or is it an ephemeral reaction to a series of temporal fortuities? Perhaps over-consumption was a result of advertising persuasion and unmeasured borrowing potential? Why is there now incapacity to pay off the loans which subsequently default? Why similar conditions occurred after Second World War in many other countries of different latitude and longitude of the planet? Remember our grandparents who thought it necessary to "Put something aside for a rainy day" and rarely were taking loans even to build a house. So there is a change of thought and institutions and the way they are expressed? They are expressed in the simple fact that fifty years later the grandson of the same grandfather now buys with a very large loan an over-sized house that he does not need and will be pressed for a very long time to repay. The grandson does not stop there and buys a car (which is made much beyond the specifications he needs) to impress the social circle. He also buys clothes and travels, and even pays the everyday expenses with credit cards. The need to have? Largely, no! Where is the eco-thinking to reduce waste of resources? Without question there are multidimensional contradictions in a global, barrier-free environment where actually it is reasonable for social contradictions to occur. Many of them are derived from a psychological deficit and crude over-consumption, which of course leads to a higher production level, but for products and services that may not be needed[97].

However, these economic differences one could say that they have their own dynamic of self-sustainability often linked with the culture of a place. The modern young man learns that he should have right from the first job financial independence including an automobile and home. That professional success is five years after starting to work and having a swimming pool and boat. That real success is to have expensive toys and financial comfort.

---

[97] Michael Mandel, How real was the prosperity? *BusinessWeek,* February 4, 2008, pages 24-27.

Perhaps the observer from a distant star would find that this is fundamentally immoral and expensive yachts, private planes, imperial weddings, luxury clothes and sumptuous meals give only superficial satisfaction while squandering wealth sources. The observer from another, equally distant star, perhaps he found that this dynamic of self-sustainability may be the cause of social progress.

And yet, the most distant observer would see that the local economic realities, and therefore all the socio-cultural aspects of a country, are approached in the light of local needs and priorities. There is a global system, a common approach.

The United States, for example, lowers the dollar interest rates because primarily the economical revival concentrates on the recovery of domestic market demand, while Europe increases its euro interest rates, desiring the empowerment of its common currency[98].

In conclusion, the question dealing with issues of information and knowledge brings us back to the topic of interest. The environment of hyper-capitalism is a natural outcome of globalization, very low cost labor, over-consumption of unsaturated consumers, social realities, not so ethical business practices and great national disparity economic conditions.

Pro-capitalism, in effect hyper-capitalism is determined by the continuous accumulation of the planet's wealth in fewer and fewer super-capitalists whilst reducing global labor cost with more people falling below the poverty line, working with the global minimum wage and producing higher quantities of products at lower costs.

In addition many argue that globalization is the primary cause of high unemployment recorded during the last decade in developed countries of Western Europe and North America with all the jobs off-shored and outsourced in low cost labor countries primarily in Asia.

---

[98] See Peter Coy, Housing Meltdown, *BusinessWeek*, February 11, 2008, pages 42-46. Observe, however, potential changes. As this text is going to print (February 2015) the Europeans Central Bank considers issuing a 1.3 trillion new euro money; the announcement alone created a 11-year low of euro against $.

This is a modern phenomenon that is the natural culmination of social, ethical and economic conditions. Still there is research evidence, which we will discuss next, of the many benefits of globalization to the poor of the world.

Hence hyper-capitalism would not have been possible without globalization and the insatiable consumption for consumers. The question is whether all these are noble, ethical and moral goals. One possible answer includes a key part of the response to address this issue by providing ethical education to train future leaders of business and even future leaders of the world[99].

One of the benefits of hyper-capitalism for the poor people is that it reduces their cost of living by making available most manufactured products at much lower prices. However, there is additional evidence of associations between globalization and poverty. In the research literature two globalization measures have been studied, trade and international capital flows. According to these studies another benefit of globalization is the economic assistance of the poor since poor countries have a comparative advantage in producing goods that use very low cost unskilled labor. Furthermore the poor are more likely to share in the gains from globalization as long as there are assistive and complementary government policies including affordable interest loans and credit to farmers, human capital and infrastructure investments, trade and foreign investment to develop exporting sectors. Unfortunately, even the favorable to the poor globalization studies also state that financial crises are very costly to the poor and globalization creates both winners and losers among the poor. Therefore there is an increased need for carefully targeted safety nets for the poor affected by globalization[100].

Transnational organizations and agreements

---

[99] See Petratos, Panos, Oxford Round Table invited speech, Nomothesia, noogenesis and noocleptia, the diamorphosis of copyright law for digital intellectual property in cyberspace, Exeter College, Oxford University, Oxford, UK, May 23-27, 2008,, and, Ritzer G. (2001) *Explorations in the Sociology of Consumption: Fast Food, Credit Cards and Casinos*, Sage Books.

[100] Ann Harrison Globalization and Poverty: An Introduction, Chapter in National Bureau of Economic Research book Globalization and Poverty (2007), Ann Harrison, editor (p. 1 - 32) Conference held September 10-12, 2004

Published in March 2007 by University of Chicago Press

Following the Second World War the Soviet Union and the United States of America formed the leadership powers of our planet. The former great colonial powers and empires began to fade and Germany, Italy and Japan were forced the roles of defeated warriors.

By the end of the war a climate of renewed optimism dominates everyone, new markets are created and many investments are initiated, many of them in other countries, far away from the home of the parent investment corporations. There is also a tendency for reduction of economic barriers and the liberalization of labor markets, deregulation of international capital transfers and liberalization of the world supply of all types of raw materials and technology transfers.

At the same time, it is clear that the former major colonial powers no longer have the authority they had. Algeria becomes independent of French domination, the British give independence to their colonies, and scientists make great technological achievements, such as Sputnik[101]. Such feats are achieved by the new superpowers. It is perhaps time to review a policy in force from the genesis of the world: Among states that have commercial compatibility or geographical affinity there should be commercial truce and socio-cultural differences should be left aside for the mutual economic interest. The power is "in unity". The global institutions like GATT and then WTO, contribute to further reduce older trade barriers[102].

The ground is therefore fertile to begin intergovernmental agreements of various types. From agreements which regulate aspects of shipping, taxes and insurance, to agreements between countries to enable the creation of common markets. Of course, today, the most important examples of such commercial groups are the country members of the European Union (28 countries) and North America (including USA, Mexico and Canada, known as NAFTA). But there are others, some of which began in the 1960s to acquire their own momentum. The global village has become much more neighborly due to these agreements. For example, most international trade is now with dollars, euros and yen. Italian lire,

---

[101] Sputnik was the first man made creation that people have sent in orbit around the world to collect information from space. The satellite was launched by the Soviet Union just over 50 years ago, in 1957!

[102] GATT stands for General Agreement on Tariffs and Trade and WTO is the World Trade Organization, the World Trade Organization, the successor of GATT, established in 1993.

German marks, or French francs are no longer required.

The inhabitant of this planet may now travel with greater easy from country to country in order to live and work in well-known legal environments and be subjected to less discrimination and less socio-cultural differences, and to hope in more peaceful realities.

Information technology, media and philosophy

For a moment let's try to imagine what the business setting was approximately two thousand years ago. The rich put the slaves to work in the fields. Some of them work less hard than their masters' expectations. The penalty included very painful measures, but such a sentence was within acceptable ethical norms of that time. Consider now the business setting in our modern time. In a modern factory we can see a plethora of automation robots which assemble complex machinery. The two supervising engineers discuss the necessity of establishing a work week of 4 days and 34 hours long. In their view it is a reality imposed by life-long educational requirements and the new ethical order. Moreover, the work that people once did now can be done by the electronic robot workers.

Generalizing, one might argue that the changes we observe in our environment depend on the level of economic development, which in turn depends on the progress of technology and thereby influence the philosophical and ethical mutations. Also, one might argue that, broadly, the ethical rules and laws are imposed by the ones possessing the technology. The brave warriors could not resist machine guns and the Second World War stopped in the face of catastrophe spread by the power of the atomic bomb. By the same token, in the century of business, a technologically inferior firm cannot compete with a high technology enterprise or with a business which is highly developed in computer and information systems thereby automating its internal management or with another business that has excellent market information (databases) and business intelligence.

There is a plethora of written works on the basis of technology and philosophy, of which a component is information and, by extension, knowledge and creation[103]. For example, a scientist who according to his

---

[103] The depth on such issues is outside the spirit and objectives of this book although in the opinion of the authors it is suitable to provide stimulus to the reader who desires to

studies is a technocrat claims that "Modern science and modern technology play their own important role in the formulation of truth ... The modern quantum physics reveals behind the scenes, the unity of creation. In the visible perception our senses perceive uniqueness, diversity, variety and the hidden truth is the unity, mental and physical, with all the associated characteristics, which are love and all human values[104]". This vision is not very close to the humane considerations of this book?

We believe that for the purposes of this work, in-depth development of business ethics issues is not necessary. However necessary are some considerations mentioned in the novel "new conditions" of modern life which create different philosophical and ethical realities from those people who were accustomed to experiencing during the pre-technological era. Based on these considerations following is an excerpt from a book by Professor Panagiotis Tzamalikos, specializing in technology and philosophy correlations[105]. Some of the "new conditions" described, adapted to the requirements of the book you have in your hands, are:

- Increase of the number of people affected by the technological advances of our time. Also, the impact of these effects to others.
- The ability of man to destroy the existing natural systems with the newly gained technological power including destruction of habitat, forests, use of radioactivity, and more.
- The responsibility that humans have to create new biomedical and ecological realities (eg, genetic changes) as well as conducting experiments, and perhaps unknown effects, in order to achieve these new creations.
- The "E" technocracy ", a new form of bureaucracy that could interfere in our personal data, the overall regulatory conditions, transparency of relationships and more.

These observations, like all those discussed in this chapter, create new obligations for prudent, carefully planned strategies, to produce a valid

---

deal with the internal philosophical thought or knowledge of oneself a topic of outmost importance that would offer a future book.
[104] From his speech (civil engineering) Professor Panikos Papadopoulos' Scientist and Human Values "held at the conference organized by the Faculty of Philosophy of the Aristotle University of Thessaloniki, entitled" The future of the humanities in Greece, November 30, 2007.
[105] Panagiotis Tzamalis, *Philosophy Perspectives of Technology*, (in Greek) Thessaloniki 1997, pages 124-133.

response to the ever-changing social conditions of our time and, therefore, the new philosophical and ethical status quo.

As we discussed, philosophy and technology contain the component of knowledge. The globalization of technology leads to a convergence of philosophical positions. The societal key to success is to possess novel technology. In other words we reiterate an earlier position: Knowledge without ethics is dangerous, especially as in time there will be no communication borders; therefore, for the masses knowledge will be possible to attain and to create opportunities for rapid employment upgrading and business competitiveness in the world. Relatively small number of workers will be able to produce significant quantities of products and services, provided by using de-centralized organizations and intangible corporate structures.

The world community quickly mutated from information society to knowledge society. Attention is given to quality information. Poor quality information gives insignificant knowledge. Different knowledge is drawn from a thorough peer reviewed medical article and different from a reality show on television. Both provide some form of information. How people make use of one type, and how they make use of the other? Are we directed to a Roman model of complacency since food and our entertainment is given? Let us, however move forward... The knowledge is already the base for a society of creation. At the same time, this very information, assisted by the existence of a convenient, user-friendly and affordable technology transmission, which did not exist thirty years ago, is the basis of mutation of the social fabric. One may wonder, if we are faced with upgrading or downgrading the human being? Suffice it to say that having an indirect adjustment of the individual in a standard virtual reality we create a socially distant public, more than vulnerable to mental illness. Also, as we shall see more fully later, the impact of technological era and the media in work ethics and the work environment is critical.

Already tens of millions of people communicate through virtual diaries (blogs) and acquire, often less than reliable knowledge through effortlessly electronic encyclopedias and search engines. References to earlier papers are becoming rare. Consumers express opinions, vote, have fun and shop from home. They have much fewer social contacts than previous generations had, and monitor even the Sunday church from the armchair. The younger, essentially derivatives of a generation of children who played with Nitendo from four years old and with the PC from six years old, have already established a questionable validity philosophical basis and perception of the truth. The technology prompted social fabric of the tens of millions of people who experience a second virtual life probably has its own philosophy which is doubtful if it is based on older philosophical teachings[106]. Yet, we can calculate that in the coming technological age, the people who are now involved in high technology, computers and virtual diaries, but now are a very small percentage of the total, is likely in the future they will be the opinion leaders of the others[107].

Let us look even more simply the effects of knowledge and technology in today's global society. As in other species of the animal kingdom, human dominance largely follows a law of the jungle where in the herd or tribe the person with more skills is considered superior and is directing the others. Usually, the battle for social dominance is based on the same sensory perception that makes obvious the dominance of one over the other subjects. A bite, a stroke, a gaze, an act which suffices to create a new social situation will be introduced followed by social addiction and later will become law.

The societies of the 21st century, particularly in comparing developed with developing nations, are significantly different from the realities encountered three centuries ago. For example, the besieged can no longer, with eyes and senses understand the ferocity or the advanced technological means of the besiegers. They will not fear and will not succumb when, instead of besiegers who they can see and evaluate, from thin air appear unmanned aircraft -which are sent from 6,000 miles away and their cutting edge technology bombs are destroying land and people. The besieged and besiegers no longer see each other face to face and they cannot see the capabilities of each other. They may not assess in advance the enemy's technological superiority. The battle is unfair and incomprehensible. The ones who possess technology, information, knowledge, excel by far. They define the ethics and the law. In the end, they impose a new social

---

[106] For a description of the phenomenon of a second life [second life], see Jessica Bennet and Malcom Beith, Alternate Universe, *Newsweek*, July 30, 2007, pages 36-45.
[107] The thought is based on the notion that opinion leaders are not necessarily richer or more educated than the others, come from all walks of life. See Philip Kotler, *Marketing Management: Analysis, Planning, Implementation and Control,* Ninth International Edition , Prentice Hall International Inc., Upper Saddle River, New Jersey 1997, page 177 and William D. Perrault, Jr. and E. Jerome McCarthy, *Basic Marketing: A Global Managerial Approach*, Twelfth International Edition, Irwin-McGraw-Hill, Boston , 1996, page 227.

dynamic and new order. But does something parallel also apply to modern business forms, for profit or not?

Mutations of the institutional framework in the global village

In addition to the substantiality of questions above, which logically should affect philosophical thought and ethics of modern man, all the principles and institutions that have traditionally been obvious perhaps currently are mutated. Let's look at projections of changes in society which, in turn, are likely to require revision of the philosophical and ethical thinking.

The death of family

The family, as we know, often under the culmination of idealistic roles, consistency, love, children, grandparents, uncles, and so forth, is a source of substantial strength for the human need for socialization and aggregation. One could identify factors that operate within the family fabric. For example from a young age, the person will find that:

- The family members may be aware of their imperfections and limitations.
- The family members take clear roles, and do not accept free assignments of identity.
- Through family socialization control systems are installed in place.
- There is a complex system that is family taboo, what to do and what should not be done.

The wedding contract, or any other similar system, is a personal acceptance of an externally imposed subordination to time and social demands of another individual. This of course leaves a gap, but over time, this gap is filled by the imposed new priorities, to the point that we do not realize now there is a void. At the same time, lifestyle, we would say the living arrangements, formulates our further behavior.

The above seem reasonable and instill some principles which lasted for millennia. In addition more than 40 years ago, Cooper[108] already hypothesized roughly as follows: "The family as an entity that

[108] The arguments of this subsection were based on David Cooper, *The Death of the Family,* The Penguin Press, London 1971, pages 24-28, 46-55 and 150-151.

characterizes all social institutions, virtually destroying autonomous initiatives through limited recognition of contribution ... Over the last two centuries the family has elapsed to make a raid on a person's life ... by default the family cannot leave nothing alone ... the family is a box of television with a color, a smell, a taste, a feeling, which always remains open ... The age of the relatives is over because they enter the center of our egos ... "

The positions of Cooper refer to trends of change of institutions like the family. Moreover, statistics show that in developed Western countries more than half of marriages end in divorce. The result is the impact on the individual. In a globalized environment, isolated from the institution of family with strong technological and social interventions, the modern individual is now the focal point of the social fabric and the modern individual will also acquire smaller potential of social response, is more vulnerable to external influences, is exhibiting confusion of values, is estranged from his fellow man, restricts the scope of communication to short messages, is unable to build complex meditations, is experiencing an immaterial world wide web and media life, is facing times of depression, loneliness and mental illness.

In a previous box information item Marshall M. McLuhan referred to the requirements of our technological age. In approaching issues of environmental ethics we should reexamine a new morality, which affects the technocratic complexity of our time. Humans, creatures of habit, are accepting the media messages without sufficient screening of the quality of information involved. This might be socially dangerous for it might restrict human choices, predispositions and actions; in the reality of today's global village this might have immediate repercussions on the societal fabric, human happiness and material (only) orientation. Therefore, one might say that we are facing an era that requires a redefinition of roles and responsibilities of man to his fellow brother, to institutions and to the environment.

A planet of older people

As we saw earlier in the subsection on contradictions around us, in some developed countries the population median is already more than 42 years[109]. In most developed countries the average person will live more

---

[109] Peter Drucker, Survey of the near future: The next society, *The Economist*, November 3, 2001, pages 3-22. Consider also newer scientific advances. Following them, the May

than 80 years and there is a strong need to import manpower from other countries, usually less developed, with younger people to fill necessary gaps in employment. People will come to fill these positions and should waive their respective cultural contradictions and adopt the local culture that more age-mature citizens of the indigenous population deem approved. And here the possibility of cultural conflict is visible.

We should also allow ourselves to see other dimensions of a world of older people? Older people bring with them cultural implications which they have experienced and thus become bridges of continuity of the social fabric. They bring with them knowledge and years of experience, have connections, they are in retirement, have low requirements for rewards, know what are culture, work and commitment, they want to remain productive and therefore many times being worthy they take up jobs meant for much younger people. And yet, with them comes a growing business of products and services for this age group, such as health, travel, golf courses, etc.

Another major mutation of our era is the emerging human enterprise in all its forms. We shall deal with the respective issues at the next chapter.

2013 issue of the *National Geographic* has on its front page a baby and the statement: This baby will live to be 120. By the same token *Time,* in its February 23rd 2015 issue has on its front page a baby and the statement: This baby will live to be 142! Laura L. Carstensen, The New Age Of Much Older Age, *Time,* February 23rd 2015, pages 56-58.

CHAPTER 3

THE ERA OF THE GLOBAL CORPORATION

What you will learn in this Chapter

In this chapter you will learn ...

- About accounting recording and discrepancies.
- About the role of the global company of the 21st century and its social and ethical dimensions.
- About the corporate transition before and after the industrial revolution
- About self actualization deficits of the global managers.
- About irregularities and alazonic behaviors of corporate stockholders and stakeholders.
- About managerial perspectives due to cross-cultural differences.
- About business bribes, lawsuits, governmental regulators and corporate governance.

Introduction to Chapter 3

In the previous chapters we aimed to outline the concepts of philosophy and ethics as well as the impact of the 21st century socio-economic practices on the global village. In this chapter, and after a short discussion of the way business realities are recorded, we address our own understanding of the role of the enterprise in the 21st century[110]. Given the cultural complexities of our world the issue of business ethics becomes of paramount importance. Therefore, the maturity, ability to face dilemmas and the self-actualization potential of the global manager is further discussed[111]. In tandem with the above issues, we present several issues from managerial perspectives due to cross-cultural differences to

---

[110] Based on John Thanopoulos key-note address prepared for the 7th Annual HSSS Conference (2010), Athens Greece, "A Systemic View of the Global Corporation: A Conceptualization, an Opinion" www.hsss2011.gr May 6, 2011.

[111] Based on John Thanopoulos presentation at the annual meeting of the Association for Global Business, Newport Beach, California, November 18, 2011, "Preparing Global Managers: Attention to Self actualization Deficits."

accounting recording and discrepancies, and from business bribes, lawsuits and governmental regulators to unexpected behaviors of CEOs of large companies.

Then, at the following chapters we discuss the major business ethical dilemmas that the main stakeholders (marketplace, employees, environment and owners) of the contemporary enterprise face as well as the platform of "how to" develop codes of ethics and corporate governance principles.

Accounting business realities

Accounting is a generally accepted way of recording business activities. It serves primarily to control and manage the enterprise. Historians have found evidence of accounting efforts in Mesopotamia nearly 5000 years ago. Only in the late 15th century, Venice used the double entry method, allowing self-checking of inputted entries. Much later the introduction of electronic search capabilities imposed new approaches and facilities for registration of entries. More recently, the use of integrated enterprise resource management systems introduced the possibility of direct implementation of any business concept for any business event.

But be careful ... in an era of globalized technological accounting bureaucracy, where the results can be obtained immediately and are related to millions of people, it is necessary that the approaches are current, valid and show what is formally required--not what people with "older ideas," different ethical standards and ulterior motives think that we should have.

For example, let's visit the case of General Electric[112] and its stock calculation fifteen years ago. Dear reader, please note that, because of its business practices GE had been constantly among the world's most admired companies. In 2001, following the usual method of calculation, GE was to distribute a profit of $ 1.42 per share. The S & P, however, suggested that from this value a certain amount had to be subtracted and, therefore, not to be included in the computation concept of profit. In the calculations of the S & P the actual profitability of GE was not $ 1.42

---

[112] The approach has been proposed by the Standard & Poor's and, in our research, it is the first time (2001) that such approach was publicly broadcasted. Now, put this issue in perspective; although the concept is already old, in many parts of the world, even by today's practices, it is very advanced and projects newer business ethical standards.

but only $1.11. The concept had immediate repercussions: Thousands of pensioners who were shareholders and whose income was based on stock performance were substantially affected by an income drop of 25%.

It is not certain whether the accounting theorists may prescribe an acceptable global system of accounting standards. Practical experience has shown the industry-wide and the culture-specific difficulties in applying universally acceptable accounting standards. At the same time business competitiveness has raised the bar by establishing new levels of accounting benchmarking. Thus, in today's complex global stock markets and business exchanges, the phenomenon of tyranny of the benchmarks[113], is present whereby professional investment managers must be vigilant to the trends and ratios because if they fail to meet expected targets, they might be subject to further legal consequences.

We are relying on accounting directives which are under constant change and subject to a series of business priorities. Here ethics in accounting is crucial. It is possible, ignorance and tendency of rapid business exploitation of data to include at least systemic accounting or financial mistakes, which as investors, entrepreneurs, or mere observers, we are not able to understand.

It should be clear that the average citizen cannot understand accounting rules. Also, keep in mind that companies mistakenly classified expenditures for many years. In the case, of WorldCom, the above action is not only a simple ethical disorder. It is an essentially illegal act[114].

The society of the 21st century is far more different from those that existed prior and for which most of the philosophical and ethical texts were written. Many things have changed such as institutions, accounting concepts, conditions, intentions, capabilities. We arrived on Mars, we have possibilities for intervention in the DNA, and we have a world with far less commercial and social barriers.

On the one hand, with technocratic ethos, the boundaries of business are

---

[113] See article by Philip Coggan, The tyranny of the benchmarks, *Financial Times*, June 8-9, 2002, page 18.
[114] U.S. Securities and Exchange Commission Litigation Release No. 17866 / November 26, 2002 Accounting and Auditing Enforcement Release No. 1678 / November 26, 2002. Securities and Exchange Commission v. WorldCom, Inc., Civil Action No. 02 CV 4963. http://www.sec.gov/litigation/litreleases/lr17866.htm

legislated, although there is nothing to protect us from the present systematic legal, accounting and financial errors. According to macro-social thinking, we do not have the ability to understand the whole business economy, local arrangements and the variations presented in different environments where businesses operate. We only have a perception of part of the image. Given the many recent corporate malpractice cases, at least, the classic approaches of audit should contain a periodic change of auditors and incorporate essential responsibility of company management.

At the same time, we should be particularly careful of systemic accounting solutions which were once acceptable and allowed but should be re-examined today. For example, labor costs for repair exceed the cost of replacement, when attempting to replace non-functioning equipment with new one. This is probably a cause of waste of society's resources. Often the construction of the replacement equipment was done in countries where the per capita GDP, obviously measured in market prices, is much lower than in the developed ones, and therefore to build it multiple man hours were needed, more than we probably realize. Caution: The accounting knowledge of the past may impose a business culture addressing issues in today's society which contradicts ecological positions (wasting resources), with educational objectives (lower capacity to resolve technical issues), and so on.

On the other hand, beyond the technocratic conduct, we must consider the substance of an institution or company. It is important to look at a corporation's relations with the environment, employees, customers, owners, corporate cultures and create codes of conduct and corporate guidelines. But before we refer to the relevant issues (and corresponding dilemmas) it is beneficial to see how, in our opinion, evolving business needs influence the world of the future.

The international and socially sensitive enterprise

The human enterprise, as an institution, has always existed but today's enterprise, especially during our modern era when all business is global, has become a very important factor for social progress and political influence. One should understand that only around twenty countries have a larger GDP than the turnover of the largest global corporations.

In the last two hundred years the corporate institution has undergone mutations. Starting from business realities of a local nature, at the end of the 19th century we find the first businesses to progressively internationalize. It is the time that the Rockefellers and the Rothschilds and the industry captains emerged. After the Second World War, the business leadership of the USA, commanding sixty per cent of the 100 top global corporations, successfully serves many of the disasters the war created through its production, manufacturing and marketing might. Thirty years later the landscape changes. Of the really big corporations, only 1/3 are still headquartered in the U.S., while approximately another 1/3 is located in Europe and another 1/3 in the rest of the world.

It is important to understand the social roles that businesses played throughout history. The realities of the pre-industrial revolution in England were characterized by companies that met local demands, workers who went to work at 6am and left 12 hours later and country environments that had small regulatory function in the business domain.

At the beginning of the twentieth century working conditions have significantly improved with key tipping point the unions. The new technology creates new conditions, large-scale production is a fact, export markets are created, the administration of the human factor indicates higher productivity methods and further improvements, working conditions, training in business management is now at university level, and globalization is *ante portas*.

> Governments cannot do everything. It is time for large corporations to enter the game. Corporate managers can help develop a methodology conducive to the development of the world but at the same time to achieve corporate objectives.
>
> Klaus Schwab, World Economic Forum[115]

For 25 years we are now in the age of global business. Naturally, that does not mean that 'good' companies are everywhere, quite the opposite. In the century of global business, well organized companies usually follow the Western-advanced model; they are organized with principles of corporate governance, integrated enterprise resource planning, careful procedures, appropriate technologies, environmentally friendly, and in the interest of

---

[115] Klaus Schwab, Founder and President of the World Economic Forum, Off the Couch, Special Edition: Issues 2008, *Newsweek,* page 21.

the worker, the owner, the customer[116]. The provision, in a knowledge society, is that in the future, we would say 25-30 years from now, the business structure will abstain from the old, monolithic, hierarchical patterns and the social fabric will be much more sensitive and versatile. Also, in the authors' view, given the potential social role of any organization, now and in the future, a prerequisite of doing business will be the existence of employee and customer-oriented administration, sensitive to social causes and its code of corporate governance.

The reader can see that there is also a contradiction in terms. Milton Friedman said that the only social responsibility of business is to increase profits. Recently (2007), Robert Reich, USA Secretary of Labor under President Bill Clinton, who for many years supported that corporate social responsibility and profitability in the long term converge, states that corporate social responsibility is a dangerous social transformation that may undermine the very concept of democracy and believes that the social responsible role of business is limited. In this sense sometimes companies reduce their costs in a manner that is consistent with the achievement of 'social' objectives. Note that one of the more acceptable methodologies of successful corporations, what *BusinessWeek* called "Best Performers", was based on measured average efficiency of use of capital resources and corporate growth during the past 36 months and always was compared to the overall efficiency of the industry[117]. These criteria of the above considerations are also proposed by Friedman and Reich. Moreover, for investors who have no targets of social responsibility, there might be a cost by investing in socially responsible strategies, though there are opposing findings in related academic research[118].

---

[116] See Thanopoulos, John and LL Schkade, "Towards Global Entrepreneurialism," *North Central Business Journal*, Volume I, Issue 7, Summer / Fall 2000, pages 46-7, and Thanopoulos, John and with Charles Little, "The Brave New Global Enterprise, " *Review of Business*, Volume 20 (Number 2) Winter 1998, page 3. Robert Reich (former US Secretary of Labor), *Supercapitalism: The Transformation of Business*, Democracy and Everyday Life, Random House, New York 2007 and In search of the good company, *The Economist*, September 8, 2007, pages 61- 62.

[117] Robert Reich, *Supercapitalism: The Transformation of Business*, Democracy and Everyday Life, Random House, New York 2007 and In search of the good company, The Economist, September 8, 2007, pages 61 -- 62.For an example, see Dean Foust, The Best Performers of 2008 (The BW 50), *BusinessWeek*, April 7, 2008, page 56.

[118] Accordingly, in a study of 40 socially responsible investment portfolios it was found that there is no cost of good business conduct. See Anne-Marie Anderson ND David H. Myers, The Cost of Being Good, *Review of Business*, Volume 28, Number 1, (Special Finance Issue), Fall 2007, pages 5-13. On page 13, it states that for those investors with socially responsible goals in their utility functions, it is clear that there is no cost, and

Revisiting the role of the global company of the 21st century

The important buildings, but also the wars, arts and technological discoveries that past civilizations left us, are forms of business activities that required vision, planning, means of production, goal organization and appropriate control procedures. However, the implementation force was human activity, the unpaid work of submissive slaves. After the industrial revolution, the engine and the use of energy, multiplied the productive entrepreneurial potential of human creativity. There have been many great books prophesizing future events.

We visualize the before-and-after the industrial revolution business realities through two 'models' the first having at its center the people of power, the Pharaohs, the Kings and the Emperors, whereas the second focuses on the individual, the everyday person. At the same time the corporation is changing and becomes able to rapidly mutate in accordance to time and region-specific societal patterns.

The basic generator of social change is the person-driven social systems of philosophy, ethics, regulations, laws and justice. In essence, in our opinion, we are in front of a global village which unifies procedures and replaces the country-state authority by a corporate-driven reality.
The proposed model is an optimistic perception of a future state that capitalizes on individual talents and deeper psychological constructs. Admittedly, however, the main concern is the transitional period of the corporation, about a century long, starting around the end of World War II.

This transitional period, requiring re-formatting of the global socio-economic thought, touches many aspects of the existing ways, including abandonment of the (mostly European) 'model' of frugality; acceptance of a modified capitalist ideal and of harmonic symbiotic relations (concepts that originate in Far East); change of present status quo, reasoning of being, regulations and laws; capitalization of the information technology potential, and so on.

---

there is social benefit to investing in socially responsible investment strategies. For investors with no such goals, there is no significant cost to invest in socially responsible strategies. The study concludes there is no cost to being good.

In our view, the existing social models of development and progress existed before and after the industrial revolution.

Before the industrial revolution era

For thousands of years of human evolution the individual is reinforced by the bonds and the social support structure of the family, the society, the race, the nation, the state. The main factors of social progress depend on the environment, the resources it provides, the philosophy and principles of the culture, scientific-technological and cultural achievements of the time, and the business thinking of society. The perception of space is based on personal observation and senses. The existence of powerful and less great people is linked to the prevailing behavioral codes (eg status of a divine Pharaoh) and to the generally acceptable dynamics of relations (eg one who is losing the war becomes a slave of the winner).

During those years, business, as an institution, exists but it has not gained the importance and the momentum it has acquired in the last two hundred years. The wars and the important buildings that past generations left us are forms of business activities that required vision, planning, concentration of means of success, organization of goals and control procedures.

Yet, ultimately, country-state might, trade opportunities, economic prosperity and cultural recognition were the main elements of sovereignty of peoples. Achieving (business) objectives was teleological in nature. For example, the hardships of the workers who built the Great Wall were not inhibitors of the progress of the project.

In essence, submission to the laws, to the religious constructs and to the concept of morality was instrumental in forming the societal fabric by limiting individual freedoms. Business profits depended oftentimes on the painfully oppressed, human labor. Prophetic of future business mismanagement applications, the Revelation of John (18-23) states "*Why your merchants (Babylon) were the rulers of the earth because of the spell you put on all nations*"[119]. By extension, and for our era, the idea of "spell" could be partially seen as advertising and influence of the media

---

[119] "For thy merchants were the great men on earth: for by thy sorceries were all nations deceived" (in King James translation).

whereas the idea of "nation" appears to be analogous to modern internationalized corporations.

Please see Figure 1, with three concentric circles. It shows how business operated in the past.

Figure 1

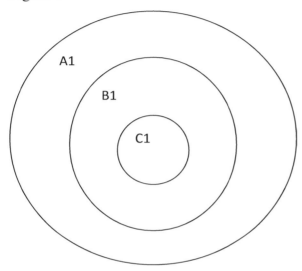

The outer circle, A1, refers to the environment and its topographical, geographical and cultural realities.

The middle circle, B1, refers to the (then) social fabric (race, nation, state) including elements such as laws, religions, procedures, science, technology, art, business, and so on.

The center of the diagram, C1, indicates the status-quo and its main systemic attention: Those in power and those who make the rules; but it does not include the ordinary people who may be considered, for all practical purposes, as slaves. In this model everybody and every system are working for the benefit, wealth and fame of those in power and of those who control the laborers.

After the industrial revolution era

Let us now move to the after the industrial revolution era …. though, please note, that in many ways the previous model still exists, especially in underdeveloped and developing regions of our planet. After the industrial revolution, the engine and the corresponding use of energy, exponentially multiplied the productive entrepreneurial potential of human creativity.

To reach their destination people no longer needed human labor to propel vehicles and vessels. The machine, powered by coal or oil, assumed this work. Thus, former rowers began using their spare time and energy to build more and better machinery and processes.

Over time, the abilities of the former rowers accelerated the rate of change. Also the former rowers (now managers) redefined systemic priorities. In redefining priorities earlier production systems were not satisfactory anymore.

After the industrial revolution any individual assumes her own rights, dynamics and reason of being. She leaves earlier from the family, divorce becomes easier, considers her own happiness and interests, she follows new norms of employment, education, material wealth, addictions and lifestyle.

As the system enables the individual to be free of restrictions imposed by family or country, the dependence on them is much less pronounced than in the past.

Of course, beyond the individual and the family, the state continues to exist but it acquires regulatory roles, both in terms of the individual's social upbringing and in terms of institutional operation, standards and controls.

One may ask: So, in your opinion, between before and after the industrial revolution, where the major systemic change occurs? Our answer is: The role of the large corporation! It now has an enhanced social role.

In fact, and unlike those who believe in a strict hyper-capitalism of financial and corporate profitability, the global corporation is now responsible for social change, production, research, development, education, and even happiness of employees.

Due to technological advances and robotized production, it is now feasible that, on a global level, the corporation can satisfy the material needs for all people.

Figure 2, again with three nested circles, illustrates, in our opinion, the role of today's global corporation.

Figure 2

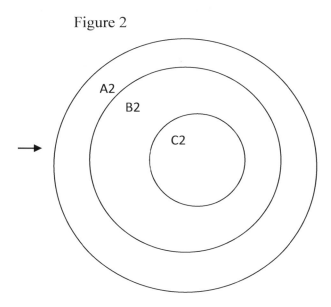

As before, the outer circle, A2, refers to the environment and its topographical, geographical and cultural realities; it adds also the complexities of the global village, a reality that allows the unconstrained move of people, products, processes, ideas and social influences.

However, the middle circle, B2, though it refers, of course, to the evolving social fabric including all previously stated elements, it has now as primary player the global corporation. This corporation is taking advantage of existing institutions, regulations, resources, national sovereignty, cultural diversity, science, technology, and so on to achieve a new social equilibrium.

The corporation is, in relation to the country-states, much less vulnerable to cultural conflict, much more flexible in social mutations of the global village, and given systems of transparent business ethics and governance, it is much more meritocratic and fair. Let's not forget that the largest 500 corporations, employing less than the 1/100 of the planet's population, produce more than 40% of the equivalent of the global Gross Domestic

Product and that the largest of these corporations have as annual turnover more than the Gross National Product of most nations[120].

Therefore, the center of Figure 2, C2, shows where the societal focus should lie: On the everyday man, whose talents, knowledge, skills and attitudes assure the corporate competitive success and its constant improvement.

Nevertheless, thousands of years of human slavery cannot change behavioral modes in just a generation. Business ethics has a pivotal role to play. A more modern understanding of the oppressed man at work is given to us by the socio-philosophical text of Urantia Book which states *"Involuntary slavery has given way to a new and improved form of modified industrial servitude"*[121].

To most people, even thirty years ago, it was an oxymoron using business and ethics in the same phrase. Nowadays, terms like business ethics, ecology or sustainability are necessary for social progress. They are also necessary conditions for the survival of human dignity, which is now independent from traditional bonds such as family, tribe or the nation. In fact, the well-managed global corporation aims to recruit talented employees and to keep them by meeting their everyday needs and their concepts of progress, education and even self-awareness.

This is not a theoretical construct. Let's offer an example: part of Canon's[122] corporate philosophy, which uses the Japanese word kyosei. A concise definition of this word would be *"Living and working together for the common good."* In fact, Canon's definition is broader: *"All people, regardless of race, religion or culture, harmoniously living and working together into the future."*

Perceptional and definitional issue: Most admired companies

Let's now move to our very present realities. Before we proceed, it is appropriate to venture to the daily usage of wording and the possible

---

[120] Annually, the *Fortune* reports on the 500 global Corporations. The last issue for the present text was published in July 21, 2014 and reports that these companies had in billions of US$ 31,058 revenues, 1,956 profits, 123,477 assets and employed 65.2 million persons.
[121] *The Urantia Book*, Urantia Foundation, Chicago, Illinois 1955, page 780.2.
[122] Accessed through www.Canon Global, April 25, 2011.

shortcomings from our inability to fully understand the intended term since the issue of ethics strongly relates to perceptional dimensions[123]. Let's take as an example the *Fortune* list of the World's Most Admired Corporations[124]. In order to define this list, "the Hay Group asked 4,104 executives, directors, and security analysts who had responded to the industry surveys to select the 10 companies they admired most."[125]

Let's take another example from the *Fortune* list of the 100 Best Companies to Work For[126]. Again it is advisable to look at the methodology used and examine if we agree with the population used for this survey, the questions asked and the knowledge of the sample to answer the questionnaires.

And then, the statistical methodologies used by the consulting "experts" of the magazine, may create a false image to the young and aspiring executive. Think of the power of the media and their capacity to impose favorable images to the everyday citizen, who may not spend the time to examine her agreement with a desired position, the essence of corporate ethics, her understanding, of the "most admired" or "the best company to work for" company. Will it be against her cultural upbringing, to lure this talented Asian young lady away from her peaceful, productive and enjoyable environment in a 40-year-long business executive dream world?

To persuade her to "move on" in spite of the fact that her brain's microchip was imprinted with a different ethical message? Don't we need a deeper understanding of the previously stated Canon's kyosei statement before we superficially impose ways of thinking and doing? Don't we need to study more philosophy and culture before we influence the modus vivendi of the people? Don't we need to better reexamine to role of the global corporation and how it will make our tiny planet a better place to live?

---

[123] From John Thanopoulos address, May 19, 2015, SEIV, Hilton, Athens, Greece on "Compliance and Corporate Governance".

[124] *Fortune,* March 1, 2015, pages 47-52.

[125] Ibid, page 52.

[126] *Fortune,* March 15, 2015, pages 60-72. Do "best performers" coincide with the "best companies to work for" or the "most admired" ones? Why? Why not? In today's world the issue of business ethics in transition is always present. Also, the reader is advised to revisit subnotes 117 and 118.

Perceptional and definitional issues: Self-actualization deficits of the global managers

From the above it is evident that in our globalized village, where international business is the key for production, standard of life, research, economic growth, even happiness of employees, we need to carefully prepare managers for a balanced experience, both in terms of functional business knowledge and in terms of personal growth. In fact, we need to consider not only the global manager, but any global citizen who, being in a position of authority, medical doctor, engineer, and so on, is responsible for the upgrading of the standard of life of the rest. Planet Earth has now seven billion people, more than twenty times its population 2,000 years ago!

We must "take care" of our global managers. Though (usually) very good in their specific fields, from a personal perspective they are very vulnerable. They cannot depend anymore on the support of their tribe, the neighborhood or the family. As individuals they have few support mechanisms. They must have self-control[127]. They think alone. They evolve by themselves. They do not have time to read the old manuscripts. They receive thousands of messages daily. They are influenced by the mass media. Moreover, given their rapid professional growth, they do not have the time to develop the survival virtues of the old aristocracy.

People teaching global business will tell you that their most difficult topic is to teach cross-cultural adaptation. Of course, there are simplistic teaching approaches, even games, but in depth understanding of the issues involved requires thorough study of local differences, philosophy, religions, knowledge of self, existential dilemmas and so on. In our very demanding global business village we should identify individuals who not only possess great subject matter knowledge, but that they have also engaged in an in-depth understanding of self. Socrates said "I am not an Athenian or a Greek, but a citizen of the world.[128]"

---

[127] Roy F. Baumeister, Conquer yourself, conquer the world, *Scientific American,* April 2015, pages 46-51.
[128] Morrison, Terri, Wayne A. Conaway and George A. Borden, *How to Do Business in Sixty Countries: Kiss, Bow or Shake Hands*, Bob Adams Inc., Holbrook, Massachusetts, 1994, page iii.

We must also see ourselves in relation to cosmos. Whereas university education develops for the last few hundred years, the Homo erectus has a relative recent presence[129] on our planet which evolved for dozens of billions of years. Consider also that our stone-age ancestors were not in a position to imagine that their great grandchildren were to invent the locomotive. Also, consider that we, ourselves, impose barriers to our thinking. For example, the U.S. Patent Office Commissioner had proposed in 1899 to terminate his office activities since "everything to be invented [had] been invented.[130]"

The primary issue with respect to the global manager lies in the world selection process. And, before that, equally important factors are organizational objectives! Assuming that modern corporations sincerely focus in "doing good" the selection of such an individual is not an easy task. Her inner strength will not be based only in cutting-edge knowledge of managerial requirements. It will be based also on her diverse knowledge, her overall philosophical background, her personal life balance and her ability to face diverse environments and dilemmas. In our opinion today's educational systems rarely support such development. Therefore, this is an independent, educational process that appears to be individual-specific. Moreover, for the individual that wishes to undertake such ventures, please understand that the motivation should not be only material. The trip in itself is the worthy experience that will allow the great enjoyment of application of philosophy, ethics and self-actualization principles.

---

[129] Of course, there is vast research on the beginnings of humans. For the philosophical interest of it, please see reference of the human of the Heidelberg tribe (Great Britain, homo antecessor-pioneer man), (*Urantia Book*, Urantia Foundation, Chicago, Il 1955, pages 719, 4-6) position supported by Pallab Ghosh, BBC News http://news.bbc.co.uk/2/hi/science_and_environment/10531419.stm, July 7, 2010. Recent findings indicate the existence of anthropoids, even 4 million years ago. Jamie Shreeve, The Evolutionary Road, *National Geographic,* July 2010, pages 34-67.

[130] Special issue of *Newsweek*, The World in 2012, September 16, 2002, page 80.

CHAPTER 4

THE MARKET AND THE CUSTOMER

What you will learn in this Chapter

In this chapter you will learn concepts that relate to business ethics and specifically ...

- About the consumer rights.
- About the concept of marketing.
- About competition, oligopolies and monopolies.
- About the safety of products.
- About contractual obligations of companies and consumer expectations.
- About the role of advertising and promotion in the modern business reality.
- About pricing and distribution issues.
- About the relationship of business ethics and market response.

Introduction to Chapter 4

Let's assume that the enterprise as a round table with three legs. One leg represents the customers the other represents the individuals possessing the capital and the third represents the employees. The customers, the capital holders, and the workers are three variables that determine the merits of each company. These variables outline the culture of the company, its philosophy and its ethical basis. If any leg of the round table is missing, the table will fall. There is also a fourth variable, the environment. Our table is standing on it.

We deal with those variables as follows: Chapter 4 is about the marketplace; chapter 5 about the employees; chapter 6 about the environment, and chapter 7, about the owners of the organization and the respective corporate governance code.

Therefore, this chapter discusses issues of ethics and business conduct with respect to the customers of the enterprise. These issues are not seen in the same way around the globe; they depend on industry, corporate size and region. Moreover, over the years we saw at least three different customer orientations.[131]

Production Orientation: Where the aim is to produce and the assumption is that the customers will "build a path" to the source of the product. In this case the producer's perspective may be: 'Make the best product you can, and people will buy it' or ' I know that people want my product '.

Sales Orientation: Where the purpose is to sell existing products, usually through aggressive sales. A typical statement of this policy is: 'sell to the customer what we have produced by making him to prefer us over the competition'.

Marketing Orientation: Where the purpose is to cover actual and future consumer needs, where the effort lies in customer satisfaction, given business objectives, and where an appropriate statement of this policy is: 'Find out what the customer wants before you make the product by using the four marketing mix variables (product-promotion-price-place) in an internally consistent way!

Theoretically the production and sales orientation were used in the past though today they are often found especially in developing regions of the world. The modern age business philosophically tends to find and meet customer needs and, in this sense, 'the customer is king' and that the rights of the client are respected. Please note that marketplace ethical issues are changing as we move among regions, industries or organizational orientation.

Consumer rights

Before 1960, even in more developed countries there were few laws that

---

[131] William G. Zikmund and Michael D 'Amico, *Marketing,* 6th Edition, South-Western College Publishing, Cincinnati, Ohio, 1999, page 17. The reader is being advised to familiarize him/herself with concepts of marketing before proceeding.

actually protected the consumer. However, in 1962 President John F. Kennedy with a unique speech to the American Congress founded the beginning of a new era. In his speech he expressed the four rights of every consumer. These were:

- The right to buy safe products,
- The right to be heard,
- The right to choose, and
- The right to be informed.

In the last fifty years, at least in developed countries, consumer rights became a reality and advanced moral-legal imperatives which were gained through social demands. Professor Peter Malliaris writes: The modern, mature, informed, satisfied, demanding, difficult, consumers should always have in mind the social dimension of consumption. Even as an individual, even marginally, with his actions the consumer can reward and punish. We must not forget and always remember. Otherwise, we lose a good producer and the bad guy wins[132].

In developed countries such rights are now obvious, although sometimes are violated. But in the largest part of our planet, these rights are not available or are systematically violated. Today, having at our disposal extensive consumer protection law statements, one could discuss a number of issues that fall within the area of consumer rights.

At the outset, however, it is necessary to emphasize that consumers should be considered just like any user of public goods and services. The consumer and citizen rights are similar to the corresponding enjoyed by any private business acting properly. We must emphasize that as a general rule, we have a public sector which often acts with bureaucratic arteriosclerosis and not in favor of the consumer criteria.

Monopolies and oligopolies

The following scheme is theoretical, and presents an ideal situation: In a market characterized by perfect competition conditions, there is an automatic tendency, that the markets converge to the point where buyers

---

[132] Peter G. Malliaris, *Introduction to Marketing*, Fourth Edition, Stamoulis Publications, Athens 2012, pages 79.

and sellers on average receive the value that they contribute[133] These conditions are:

- There are too many buyers and sellers without anyone individually enjoying an important part of the market.
- All buyers and sellers can enter and leave the market freely and directly, without cost.
- All buyers and sellers are fully aware of what's on the market, including quantity, quality and price.
- There is a similarity in products or services that do not vary in an essential way.
- Production costs are paid by producers. No other third party intervenes or takes part in production costs.
- All buyers and sellers want to maximize the usefulness (utility) of the product, minimizing the cost to them.
- Third parties, e.g. the government, do not intervene in setting prices, quantities, quality, or anything else related to the available product.

Theoretically then, a market that covers the above conditions is cost effective and high-cost businesses are eliminated. But even then, economists say that market mechanisms may fail (market failure) and, therefore, the ethics of such competition is in doubt. Examples: The efficiency of the economy has a human cost, which is often not taken into account. The burdens and difficulties of competing change are not carried equally by all. The market system does not guarantee that all receive sufficient income to be able to enjoy the benefits they want, and so on[134]. On the other hand competition realities may develop market conditions which, by design, are not always respectful of the rights of consumers. Such situations are:

Monopolies: Here we have the case that only one company owns the entire market and the customer has no choice. Either, the customer will buy the product at the price and conditions offered by the monopoly, or will not enjoy it at all. For various reasons, other companies can not enter the market. Often public companies operate, even now, as a monopoly.

---

[133] See, Velasquez, Manuel G., *Business Ethics: Concepts and Cases*, Fourth Edition, Prentice Hall, Upper Saddle River, New Jersey, 1998, pages 208-216.
[134] See William P. Albrecht, *Economics*, 2nd Edition, Prentice-Hall Inc., Englewood Cliffs, New Jersey, 1979, pages 34-39.

Usually such companies are in energy, transport, telecommunications, police, defence, health care and education. For over 100 years in the U.S., the Sherman Antitrust Act and subsequent regulations, prohibit the existence of monopolies. Recently, a similar case law has made similar arrangements in the European Union and other countries.

The monopolies were created originally either as a unique company, as in the early 20th century the Aluminum Company of America, or by mergers. A classic example of corporate mergers was Standard Oil, now ExxonMobil. For many reasons monopolies lead to imperfections. Here are some[135]:

- The accepted by many capitalist justice leads to a market which, as mentioned above, is characterized by conditions of perfect competition and where there is a tendency for markets to converge at the point where buyers and sellers on average receive the value they contribute. In a market controlled by a monopoly prices tend to be high and balance is not achieved.
- The markets work in an inefficient manner, especially regarding the distribution and supply of technology, raw materials, and so on.
- Price differentials, as the need arises for a product can create antisocial situations, such as products associated with health.

For the above reasons, as well as for other similar reasons, monopoly markets are contrary, to the spirit of capitalist justice, resource use, rights of clients. Therefore, substitution of the producer, as "king" of the market is fundamentally contrary to the acceptable ethical market.

Oligopolies: In certain markets there may be only monopolies. In the small town there is only one supermarket and only one bank. They are monopolies. But too often we encounter situations that are characterized as oligopolies. We have few sellers and for new entrants is not easy to penetrate the market. The existence of oligopolies is a function of specific situations that are enjoyed by companies involved in markets such as raw materials, technology, patents, which identify the area of the market. Examples: Gerber is recognized as the market leader for baby food, Kodak is renowned for photographic products and Gillette for razors. DeBeers controls a large share of production of diamonds. Microsoft and Intel have expertise in software and hardware of personal computers, respectively,

---

[135] Op. Cit., Velasquez, pages 222-223.

and so on. Furthermore observe that a corporate raiding or merging may result in a marketplace oligopoly or even monopoly.

Undertakings of businesses in an oligopoly have room to act in a parallel way with companies that enjoy monopolies. Also, they find it relatively easy to disguise moves which can lead to action:

- Special agreements that force retailers to stop buying from other producers to sell at specific prices, not to sell over a defined area, to grant contracts for the sale of a product but at the same time with another product, etc.
- Differential pricing (price discrimination) where for the same product under the same conditions and the same amounts are charged different prices.
- Cooperation between producers to jointly determine price (price-fixing).
- Cooperation between producers to reduce production, thus forcing retailers to sell products at higher prices.
- Informal agreements, one with each other can direct companies to antitrust actions, which determine prices or other aspects of trade between companies of the oligopoly.

It is clear that such actions may lead to irregular behavior. Note that, over the years, economists presented views with varying impact in the marketplace. For example, economists argued that an oligopolistic situation in an industry may be facing competition from another industry that requires a prudent attitude towards the customers or, as scholars of the Chicago School argued, markets can be cost effective if there are even only three companies which provide the supply or production[136].

Potentially the large global corporations are in a position to force local manufacturers to produce[137] a better and a cheaper product. They have the power to do so. They command economies of scale, have a better perception of the consumer needs, standardize processes and products world-wide and draw suitable human resources for all their focused objectives. Additionally, their governance principles, their constitution as we shall see, are already geared towards ethical behavior, the societal

---

[136] Robert H. Brock, *The Anti-trust Paradox: A Policy at War with Itself*, Basic Books, New York, 1978, pages 20-58 and 405.
[137] At this point the reader is kindly asked to review business ethics issues discussed in the first chapter.

benefit and the sustainable environment. In contrast, the localized smaller enterprise is less effective. If a small business does not play by the rules of the producers it may be expelled from the market.

Products' safety

Another area that is linked with the issues of consumer rights, is the safety of products. Almost every product we use contains a risk. Examples: A plastic bag may cause choking of a child. Smoking is harmful to health. The airbag has a better result when the passenger puts on the safety belt, and so on. Therefore, when we talk of safety of products for the consumer we mean the reasonably acceptable level of risk. Thus, the product must indicate the reasonable potential risk due to the use of the product. But be careful ... reasonably acceptable risk is not synonymous with any risk which can be avoided. Using these parallel versions of the U.S. Product Safety Commission on product safety, we can formulate the following principles[138]:

- Consumers should be aware that the risk exists.
- Even if the consumer knows that there is a risk, he is to be granted an opportunity to assess the frequency and intensity of risk.
- The consumer must know that the risk can be treated.
- The consumer should be able to evaluate the risk-cost basis. In other words, decide to reduce the risk by assuming a greater financial burden.

We would state, therefore, that the manufacturer of a product, and in expansion the seller, must be able to inform any potential buyer of these product risks, the use of the product involves. This is an area of moral responsibility, which is appropriate to work with clarity and sense of social obligation, even if no corresponding legal wording exists that refers to what is the way forward in an accident, the incidence of risk, and so on.

---

[138] See Lowrance, William W., *Of Acceptable Risk*, William Kaufmann, Inc., Los Altos, CA 1976, page 80, and referencing *The Final Report* of the National Commission on Product Safety where the previously mentioned principles are presented from their negative side.. Manuel G. Velasquez, *Business Ethics: Concepts and Cases,* Fourth Edition, Prentice Hall , Upper Saddle River, New Jersey, 1998, page 329.

Contractual obligations

The fact that there may be legal sanctions because of breach of contract does not redefine the business ethical obligation to consistency in the promising statements. Generally we would say that the corporation, bringing a product to the market delivers an indirect contractual obligation to comply with the following requirements[139]:

- The product truly delivers what it promises it offers as regards to the specifications, reliability, warranties, the possibility of maintenance and service, and reasonably foreseeable safety during use.
- The transaction is clear and transparent. The manufacturer offers any information necessary to enable the consumer to have a clear picture of the product purchased. Example: A claim that in our geriatric unit we have medical supervision is not enough if we only have a contract switching patients to a neighboring hospital facility, or if our office is open only certain hours a day.
- There are transaction formalities which are true. We mentioned the 'sales orientation' where there may be a culture 'not looking at what the customer is looking for-we sell it'. Falsehoods and 'white lies' are commercial realities both in underdeveloped and developed countries. Business ethics considers as a necessary condition the elimination of deliberate commercial falsehoods and establishes methods to prevent false operations.
- Do not allow the oppression of the consumer. Commercial approaches may be forcing the buyer to purchase a product that would not buy under other circumstances. Experienced vendors can take advantage of the psyche, the fear or the pressure that the consumer receives the product a certain time. These tactics are incompatible in a sense of business ethics.

At this point there should be a clarification. Can marketplace promises be realized, kept or even measured, and then, by whom? Let's take as an

---

[139] For contractual obligations of the company, see ibid. The Contract view of Business's duties to consumers, pages 326-334. For example, the seller must give the client adequate and focused attention on consumer services' by providing competent and customer-focused sales and service. See parallel notions at Insurance Marketplace Standards Association and the IMSA Code, Thomas C. Reischi, *Ethics and Customer Service,* National Underwriter, Cincinnati, Ohio 1999, page 84.

example that the retailer sells a washing machine with a ten-year warranty. Can the grandson of the old lady who bought it figure out where his grandmother kept the receipt or even who was the retailer who sold it? This raises an even more serious issue of ethical responsibility in keeping a promise.

Usually we put the products and services on a conceptual straight line of hierarchy, which at one end are intangible services, e.g., a theatrical performance, a haircut, or offering an MBA, and at the other end are tangible products, e.g., cement or types of wood. The very broad intermediate area of the conceptual hierarchy also includes all products that have both tangible and intangible elements. For example, eating food at a good restaurant, purchasing a shirt that has a familiar logo, or purchasing a machine with a warranty.

Generalizing, as we move towards intangible products, manufacturing more complex products, expensive products, luxury goods and their respective combination of products, the harder it is to meet the exact specifications promised to consumers. Therefore, consumers are more vulnerable to non-ethical business operations if the operator has to arrange everything and apply his limited understanding of business ethics.

Advertising and promotion issues

One of the four variables of marketing, is advertising which includes promotion. Without advertising and promotion, the product cannot be known and therefore cannot be in demand, which in turn will help reduce its overall cost. At the same time advertising creates a quasi-monopoly. Habitual behavior works as a second nature *forcing* buying decisions. Branding therefore represents a significant value to the corporation. Consumers recognize the products of famous corporations, for example, Nike, Nikon and Nokia and therefore tend to rely on them for a next purchase. Of course, companies are trying, through advertising, to create connections of consistency, quality, ethics and good business practice, so when consumers acquire their products and services, consumers meet precise needs through these services and products.

In this area marketing research plays a very important role, focusing its attention in the particular segment(s) of interest. Demographics, psychographics and consumer behavior information give a clear picture of consumer needs as it relates the target consumer and its potential buying habits. The corporations, providing the means and expertise for research, offer just what attracts consumers' attention, to convince her and make her buy the product or service. It is not essential that the products of an acceptable and properly advertised franchise with an alleged high number of restaurants are better or tastier than the local taverns.

Still, some analysts will tell us that advertising is often wasting resources (wasteful) and others will say that advertising offers a market power which the small retailer cannot have. It is often the argument that advertising, as well as any promotions, are designed to create desires, which may lead to higher consumption and growth of an independent production system. Indeed, several decades now, scientists argue of the validity of John Kenneth Galbraith perception that the purpose of advertising is to manage and shape the consumer, which probably leads to restriction of choice and free will[140]. The machinations of advertising and promotions of products limit the buying habits of consumers. So the consumer accepts the superiority of a product because of a well-known brand and is whiling to pay the highest price, without being able to distinguish that the same product of less known brand at two higher shelves, is much cheaper and equally well covers her needs.

Furthermore, the approaches and promotional products potentially not only reduce the buying habits of consumers, but also indirectly drive makers and market channels. Are we really confident that the advertising approaches are used at the global level and through the internet, morally neutral, ethical and objective?[141] For example, according to Professor Adriane Fugh-Berman a minute long discussion and a lot of free samples of medicines is sufficient, to allow a medical pharmaceutical representative to get a doctor to prescribe a particular drug and thus to increase its sales of the medicine by 16%[142]. Is this an ethical practice?

---

[140] John Kenneth Galbraith, The New Industrial State, New American Library, New York 1967, page 211.

[141] See Emmanuella Plakoyiannaki, Kalliopi Mathioudaki, Pavlos Dimitratos, Yorgos Zotos, Images of Women In Online Advertisements of Global Products: Does Sexism Exist? *Journal of Business Ethics*, Spring 2008.

[142] Case in point: To reduce the practice of medical representatives in the United States more than $20 million have been given to at least thirty academic Professors to prepare appropriate lessons and case studies which hope to reduce the tendency of doctors to dutifully accept the advice of medical representatives and to see under a more critical

Has advertisement a potential of not being ethical by affecting the consumer buying behavior?

Problems in pricing and product distribution

It makes sense to have ethical dilemmas in each dimension of the marketing mix and a variety of views such as those practiced in each profession. As in any of the cases of the dilemmas presented in this book, also here according to the writers, a panacea is not proposed. Simply we enter the debate and it is for the reader to handle the presented case at will. Let's see some examples:

Credit and lending is part of the overall pricing policy. We are at the beginning of 2000 and our client opts for a beautiful country house and believes it is time to have her dream. Given the total demand, the price of the house is considerably more expensive than foreseen ten years ago. But there is a general spirit of economic optimism.

The imposed new debt required that the purchase is based on the mortgaging of her shares. The banker who conducted the transaction has some misgivings about the future of the economy, but says nothing. For the bank the transaction is guaranteed. The customer has confidence in her investments. So both parties move ahead and secure the relevant loan. Three years after the stock market equity investment of the client has lost a significant part of the value and performance of stocks is negative. The customer cannot repay her obligations and loses the beautiful countryside home and the remaining investments. Were the banker's actions ethical?

In many developed countries for many years we have become accustomed to cheap and easy money through credit cards offers. With credit cards we are buying products as a pair of shoes or a TV, things that have a direct physical sense. However we continuously charge cards with our intangible costs, such as restaurants, hairdressers, travel, plastic surgery, vacations and so on. We cannot remember when, nor why we spent an amount, but each month a payment must be paid to credit card bills because we will lose the possibility of further borrowing. Statistics show that a good

---

perspective such promotions. It is noteworthy that the funding of such courses came from a twenty five times fine imposed in 2004 to a known pharmaceutical corporation for use of inappropriate marketing methods. See Ariene Weintraub, Just Say No To Drug Reps, *BusinessWeek*, February 4, 2008 page 69.

number of consumers pay their credit cards immediately. The others are charged interest and a significant proportion of them find difficulty in repaying those debts[143]. With credit cards a consumer can make cash withdrawals that banks lend quite easily. Perhaps over-consumption is not a social virtue? Should companies follow the same policies of conduct, to switch to more conservative tactics, even if it means lower sales? How does this sound in terms of business ethics?

Our grandparents were accustomed to a transaction directly with your local dealer or shopkeeper. There was a transaction and return to their daily lives. In the post-war era, a revolution in retail occurs ... purchasing products and services come with luxury establishments which offer, besides satisfaction with the product itself, a total experience where the consumer is experiencing this environment to the point it becomes a habit the frequent visit to it.

Perhaps, there are other social implications because of the time required to go to this purchasing location downtown, for example whether it deprives us of time from family or from going to a museum? Is ethically acceptable to abruptly change long established social behaviors by indirectly serving personal ego desires and, at the same time, business objectives?

Mrs. Indra Nooyi is born in India and is CEO of PepsiCo, and envisions the company to offer continually more foods that are good for health (good for you) of the consumers. The thought of it started in the mid-90s when the then CEO of PepsiCo has been asked to create a corporate strategy for the 21st century. This was followed by an overall shift in marketing based on corporate awareness, proper nutritional needs of the future and effective corporate social responsibility.

Note that the company does not have only the well-known Pepsi cola, but also thousands other products such as Doritos, Frito-Lay, Taco Bell, Pizza Hut, Kentucky Fried Chicken, Tropicana Juices, Gatorade, etc.[144].

---

[143] Mara de Hovanesian, Christofer Palmeri, Nanette Byrnes, and Jessica Silver-Greenberg, Over the Limit, *BusinessWeek*, February 18, 2008, pages 34-43.
[144] Betsy Morris, The Pepsi challenge: Can this snack and soda giant go healthy?, *Fortune,* March 3, 2008, pages 42-50. For data updating, see also Global 500 where PepsiCo stands as the 137 for 2013 largest global corporation with revenues exceeding 66 billion US$, profits 6.7 billion US$, managing assets in excess of 77 billion US$ and having 274,000 employees. *Fortune*, July 21, 2014, page F-3.

Products of questionable value and social tolerance

In a previous subsection Galbraith has criticized the advertisement saying that advertising may limit choice and free will of the consumer. What should you think about an entire company or an industry segment of companies which capitalize on the poorly understood consumer addiction? Addiction obliging him, largely against his will, to buy again and again the products or services of one particular company? For example, let us consider the reason for the existence of companies producing cigarettes or alcoholic beverages or companies that operate gambling centers? Is there an ethos to such companies, why, why not? In order to avoid criticism of present wrongdoings, let's consider past practices for the case of casinos[145].

Americans spent enormous amounts of dollars in various gambling activities. This amount is greater than what they spent in the sports arenas, cinemas and theme parks, such as Disney World, Seven Flags, or Sea World. Undoubtedly, there is a fun element but also a spending addiction. Is this an ethical business practice and an acceptable societal mode to build tax revenues?

Of course, like any well-organized corporation, know-how plays an important role here. In American casinos an atmosphere conducive to playing and gambling is created. The atmosphere is based on free drinking and intense noise. In contrast, in Europe a philosophy is followed that allows the player to calm down and concentrate. Perhaps that is the reason in America people spend more money on gambling than in Europe.
One could say that if a society considers something as unethical, it can record it in law as legally unacceptable. Maybe! Maybe?

And yet ... you remember this itinerant vendor of music CDs. Selling his wares so cheap that people bought from him all the CDs but rather it was clear that these products were only infringing copyright. Or you remember the company that advertised on the Internet that sells "replicas" of well-

---

[145] The source is Richard C. Morais, The stakes get higher, *Forbes Global*, April 29, 2002, pages 24-27; according to the same source gambling in America is 1% of consumption, in Asia and the Middle East is up to 1.8%, in Australia and New Zealand 5.5%. This percentage in Europe is 0.4% with the exception of England which is 0.9%. The average for the world is 1% of consumption expenditure. Figures from this sub-chapter are coming from the same source and from others that Morais led us. However, and for comparative purposes all of them refer to the same period.

known watches and expensive gifts; Are the "after-market" markets illegal? -markets that are selling the true object, but not through the "authorized dealer" and often with very high discounts[146].To make clear how complex the issue is, consider a factory that manufactures products of an international brand name. The same factory may, during hours of non-operation, and with failure of supervision, produce additional similar products to move to different channels. According to the firms that produce and legally own the intellectual property of such products this shadow manufacturing process is illegal and only adds to business profit loss, corruption, smuggling and global tax evasion. What is the reason behind all these? The human limitless desire for luxury and excess.

For example, there are famous auto manufacturers that in their top 2015 models have "more than 100 electric motors power bleeding-edge systems ...."[147]. Do we really need all these gimmicks? Do we understand their repercussions? Is the production of excess truly ethical?

Let's see some other examples of products of questionable value legally permitted or which social tolerance allows the existence of:

- Is it right to have arms-producing companies? What will we tell the old lady who has invested her little money in the fund "X" if she learned that some of her money is invested in the company of weapons "Y" which manufactures the rifles with which they killed her sons at war?
- What would we tell the popular businessman, trying to upgrade his business, and without knowing much, hires a new recruit with a "masters" in business administration when, retrospectively, the business owner realizes that the recruit's degree was not based on "new knowledge" but that the "masters" was credited based on previous professional experience and that this was the key to give the new educational qualification of a postgraduate degree;
- What would the majority of the world think if they learned that the acceptance of some awards or subscribing to a "who's who" require the payment of any amount?
- Would you assume the position where you are a retailer, of a company which bases its sales on the use of your network, a kind

---

[146] For a brief analysis of this issue, see Sarah Murray, The fight against fakes is far from over, *Financial Times*, 6-7 April 2002, page 5.
[147] Sue Callaway, A Car, and Then Some, *Fortune,* March 15, 2015, page 16.

of marketing which is based on creating a "pyramid" of personal relationships with likely cost the loss of some friends?

The fact is that the availability of a product through pyramidal marketing, accepting a prize (which was achieved because someone paid the prerequisite amount) at a special celebration, providing a masters which does not cover the expected subject matter, the sale of weapons or lottery, have become socially and legally acceptable actions. So the question remains: Are these examples of social tolerance in a questionable activity, or addiction to a self-destructive habit like smoking is a matter of morality and ethics that the business world needs to address and regulate itself? Or that the whole industry should face this issue in a way that equally contributes to the overall social cost, which might otherwise be unfairly charged to the average taxpayer? At the same time, however, shouldn't the consumer be allowed to choose and buy as much as he wants? These are questions that shareholders must resolve before establishing a business of questionable social value. There are people who would not want to invest or work for it, as there are people willing to invest in any profitable business purpose.

Requiring the 'total' product

In the past forty years, the consumers, particularly those of developed countries have realized that they have certain rights regarding their products and services used. The philosophy of marketing has been crucial to the upgrading of consumer rights.

Let's see a couple of examples:

*   Worldwide operations focused their interest in innovative products in line *with environmental positions, such as hydrogen electric vehicles or* sustainable nature powered energy production, even capitalizing on the sea waves to produce electricity[148].
*   What about, cases such as the Société Générale, which led to losses of 7.5 billion U.S. dollars due to the actions of a young employee (trader), conclude that any firm must not only have great balance sheets, but also quality and unparalleled relationships regarding investors (ie, customers of

---

[148] Telis Demos and Peter Gumbel, Eight Great Green Ideas, *Fortune*, April 28, 2008, pages 42-48 and Anne Underwod, 10 Fixes for the Planet, *Newsweek*, May 5, 2008, pages 50-52

the bank), press (i.e., sincere arguments outwards) and institutional organizations (ie, legal and governmental framework)?[149]

Let us therefore return to the definition of marketing. We must provide our consumers the desired product or service at the right time, at the right price, with the appropriate distribution and following promotions and views that give the right information and the desired image. At the same time overall practices and procedures that our organization follows must be within acceptable ethical limits set by the consumer within our moral and ethical framework.

Consumers, especially in developed markets, are now clear about their rights to the point that if justice is not served, further compensation is given as consumers are not satisfied with merely a simple refund. Vigilant, going to judicial solutions, they are looking to find ways to punish the company that offers the unfulfilled promises.

The requirement for a "total" product to offer the guarantees of security, true standards, sound advertising and promotion of consistency with contractual obligations, freedom of choice, and so many others we have seen in this chapter is motivated by our entrepreneurial era and modern social imperatives.

Nowadays the consumer wants to acquire a particular product but also is directly influenced by the business culture of the organization we represent. The business culture indicates how the agency is thinking about the ecology, the environment, employing young employees, the exploitation of natural resources. All these are in the field of business ethics but also in the area of good business strategy.

We conclude this chapter and the topics we discussed about markets, customers and marketing, with an observation: Particularly in wealthy countries, and given an inclination to leisure, media proliferation and inability to focus on philosophical positions creates an artificial sense of self-indulgence for virtually nonexistent over-consumption needs.

The man, a being of addiction, learns to fill his time with purchases of things and services that are not needed, which essentially make him socially more vulnerable and in turn increase the apparent output of the

---

[149] Peter Gumbel, Saving Société Générale, *Fortune*, April 28, 2008, pages 42-48.

economy. The wealthy, from the comfort of his personal space, it is very difficult to feel the needs of billions of people living in unbearable financial conditions. For them, our fellow humans on Planet Earth, the concept of a "total" product is different. These underprivileged people just want simple houses, basic transport, few clothes, some information and basic medical care. The others demand palaces, expensive French dresses, jewelry, cosmetics, fast sports cars, trash magazines, online platforms for personal confirmation of their ego, or plastic surgery beauty. If we understand basic human needs and allocate appropriate for their case products, the global production machine remains fully employed, and there will not be a waste of resources and we will provide social contribution. Perhaps, then, we should systematically turn to the profitable business of producing and marketing "total" products for the developing markets? After all perhaps thereby we will achieve key objectives of business ethics.

And yet, perhaps in the future we find ourselves in a situation where the consumer "needs" of people will not always identify what to be produced and marketed, where pro-social and pro-ecological factors will institutionally limit the potential of consumer choice and where, in parallel meaning of "patriotism" of earlier eras, consumer restraint is still a social virtue. But then, one may ask: Are these new era dogmatic postures, in effect limiting human freedom, reason of existence and ethical perception?

CHAPTER 5

THE CENTER OF OUR ATTENTION: THE EMPLOYEES!

What you will learn in this Chapter

In this chapter you will learn concepts that relate to the workplace ethics, and specifically ...

- About the modern worker and how that role developed in the past fifty years.
- About the increase and upgrade of the role of the female worker.
- About issues on retirement and people with disabilities.
- About new educational realities.
- About work "principles" and quality of life.
- About the principle of balance in the rights and responsibilities of workers and employers.
- Workers' rights and responsibilities.
- Rights and responsibilities of employers.
- For the roles that employees have and potential conflicts due to these.

Introduction to Chapter 5

In the previous Chapter we talked about the fundamental element of business, the customers! If there are no markets there is no reason for a business to start. May we remind you, dear reader, that metaphorically speaking we represented business as a three legged stool: Customers, employees, owners! The stool stands on another variable, the environment. Any leg cut means that the stool falls. This Chapter deals with the employees, the next with the environment and the Chapter 7 with the owners of the corporation, finance and the respective code of governance.

In this chapter, having reviewed a general description of trends taking shape around the modern worker, we discuss the rights of workers and employers, as well as the "balance" between the two. We live in an ever-changing globalized reality. Before 1800 the worker, usually, was captive of feudal lords' rules and regulations. With the industrial revolution new labor rules were imposed. Even today management often needs to answer

the Machiavellian ethical dilemma: To be feared or to be loved?[150]
Moreover, what about when people in Nepal offer glorification to a nine

---

[150] A doctoral student at the University of Piraeus, Fanis Tseperkas, contributed the following note about The Ethical Dilemma - To be feared or loved? His source is primarily Ricci Luigi, Machiavelli Niccolo: The Prince, Institute of Medieval Studies, 1943, Toronto, Canada.

> But such as love me, guard me of their tongues. [..] Admir'd I am of those that hate me the most; [..] though some speak openly against my books, yet they will read me. [..] let them know that I am Machiavelli. The Jew of Malta.

Via a Machiavellian viewpoint, whatever action related to the welfare of the State or Enterprise, is well-founded, no matter how adverse it might seem, given a socio-economic reality characterized by corrupt leaders, poorly designed institutions and people tending to wickedness and egoism. Consequently the issue of Necessity refers to what is humanly necessary in parallelization to what is necessary for the fulfillment of humanly needs. Via a Machiavellian perspective, it becomes a justification for the acquisition of what is considered necessary regardless of the morality of the process in acquiring them with the motivation to act accordingly, stemming not from within the Prince or Manager, but from the reality or circumstances he might be opposed with. Therefore the virtue of a Prince or Manager, for Machiavelli is the product of the process of developing prudence for the sake of the necessity of security of the State.

At this point the question "and what would the practical meaning of these admonitions to today's entrepreneurial practice be?" would be justified.

The answer is provided via a Machiavellian perspective in the lines to follow. Prior to materializing any of the admonitions to follow, the reader is advised to take into consideration, philosophical, legal and environmental dimensions.

Due to the very concept of Necessity stemmed, the most controversial dilemma Machiavelli has posed through his work -which led him to carve his own space in history. A Prince or Manager ought to be loved or feared? Relevant is the following part of Machiavelli's work (page 66): *"[..]The reply is that one ought to be both feared and loved, but as it is difficult for the both to go together, it is much safer to be feared than loved, if one of the two has to be wanting."*

And proceeds to reinforce the previous argument as follows: *"[..]for love is held by a chain of obligation which, men being selfish, is broken whenever it serves their purpose; but fear is maintained by a dread of punishment which never fails"*

The cornerstone of Machiavelli's admonitions is summarized within the previous lines. According to him the Prince has one and very specific duty, a single purpose which he will either succeed at enjoying the gratitude of his immediate environment or fail suffering the dismay of his subordinates.

It is hence clear that a "Prince" or manager should aim to achieve both as far as his environment is concerned. Still, should any of the above be found wanting, the manager should aim at the type of fear that is translated into obedience and strategic behavior.

Moreover, research interestingly has shown that fear of failure is one of the most motivating forces among managers.

Moreover, research interestingly has shown that fear of failure is one of the most motivating forces among managers.

years old girl believing that her eyes draw the beholder into direct contact with divine[151]? Does this change their predisposition towards ethical issues? And then, going back to feudal lords' rules and regulations, who is imposing today's the legal conformity and why the average citizen should blindly respect, for example, the protocol towards a Queen or a Pharaoh.

Let's move forward when nowadays, it is possible for the employee to be the manager of a factory of robots, of a super-tanker carrying 300,000 tons of oil, or of a wire transfer of millions of dollars in an hour, hence the choice, responsibility, knowledge, renewal of the worker acquires completely different dimensions than before.

Of course, we continue to consider issues about the rights or choice or education or work environments for employees. Facing and attempting to resolve these associated dilemmas, trade unions are pushing legislators to improve working conditions. We observe, however, the existence of a new business reality. The progressive global companies of the world, trying to identify the best executives, spare no cost. They offer their employees much more than what is guaranteed by law. The perks offered include but are not limited to gyms, gourmet cuisines, travel and thus create an effective culture of loyalty to corporate goals. As previously, we concluded that business ethics for the market and the customer is synonymous with the principles of proper marketing, so we will have to conclude that the inspired management of human resources goes beyond the moral rights or legal obligations: It's a business necessity to attract talent and, in turn, the new business talent will achieve corporate objectives.

Workers of the 21st century

In the recent history of earlier cultural images there are family models of Western style where the main producer of work and income earner is the father of the family and where specific roles are held by the mother, grandparents and children. There are also specific expectations from the first born, the older sister, and so on[152].

---

[151] Isabella Tree, Living Goddess of Nepal, *National Geographic,* June 2015, pages 78-97.

[152] For example, let us bring in our minds, as a model of a Western-style family, movies of the decade 1950-1960, somewhere in France or the U.S., where the father leaves in the morning for work which brought the family the primary income, provisions of their livelihoods and social value, while the mother stays back to care for the home and to raise

Furthermore, in another country where polygamy is permitted, the father may have four wives, and thus can procreate a lot of children. Again there are working and non-working roles and expectations of all family members. And the roles and expectations are a function of socio-economic conditions and to some extent we are witnesses to an era when perhaps could be characterized by the phenomenon of death of the institution of family. A function of parallel socio-economic conditions is that the realities of the workplace change. Thus, entering the 21st century and a plethora of employment opportunities in Western-type societies, we see certain trends, like the role of the female worker, the elderly, people with disabilities, education and quality of life. Obviously, similar factors affect the philosophical and ethical predispositions of each and every social cohort.

Trends of a new era

The after the industrial revolution era did not only free the capable to work enslaved man. It gave a new social status to the underprivileged, promoted education, changed the role that women had in the work force, established standards of life quality, allowed the worker "to reach his full potential" … well, not as yet always! In summary, work trends maybe described as follows:

Enhancing the role of the female worker: In the last fifty years, the social role of women has changed. Previous conditions and the ensuing result of this change are to enhance the capabilities of various jobs. Females become the leaders of large countries like India or England, they take over the administration of large companies , they are lawyers, doctors, university professors, members of parliament, senators, congress persons, ministers and prime ministers, and, often, a female earns more money than her husband. Of course a woman's requirements of her working environment are upgraded as well.

In addition, consider the fact that that this evolution has happened only very recently. For example, the most famous military school-university in the world is West Point. The tradition required to enroll only men. In May 1980, the first 61 American women officers graduated from West Point. Gender roles and the times change[153].

---

her children and to work on some charitable projects. Usually when the female spouse works she does so in a less income productive work than her partner.

[153] James Salter, It's not the old Point, Life Magazine, May 1980, pages 70-79.

In addition, consider the fact that that this evolution has happened only very recently. For example, the most famous military school-university in the world is West Point. The tradition required to enroll only men. In May 1980, the first 61 American women officers graduated from West Point. Gender roles and the times change[154].

Presently it has become trendy for companies to boast publicly about their efforts to provide more female-friendly perks. Increased maternity leave (both paid and unpaid), telecommuting, job sharing—the list goes on …. The underlying goal? To attract and retain the best female talent[155].

The average retirement age increases: In the last 100 years there have been medical scientific revolutions. This led to the significant increase in human longevity. In the U.S., for example, in 1900 the average life span just exceeded 47 years and 100 years later was close to 77[156]. The extension of human life certainly has created new employment opportunities. Is also essential that contributes to the conservation, continuation and adaptation of corporate culture to changes in the modern world, capitalizing on the experience and wisdom usually older business veterans can offer.

The average retirement age increases: In the last 100 years there have been medical scientific revolutions. This led to the significant increase in human longevity. In the U.S., for example, in 1900 the average life span just exceeded 47 years and 100 years later was close to 77[157]. The extension of human life certainly has created new employment opportunities. Is also essential that contributes to the conservation, continuation and adaptation of corporate culture to changes in the modern world, capitalizing on the experience and wisdom usually older business veterans can offer.

People with disabilities: A paraplegic had little opportunity to be productive in a useful manner at the beginning of last century. The conditions in the world have dramatically improved, especially because of

---

[154] James Salter, It's not the old Point, Life Magazine, May 1980, pages 70-79.
[155] Colleen Leahey, 10 Best Companies for Women, *Fortune,* May 15, 2015, page 55.
[156] *The World Almanac and Book of Facts 2000*, Primedia Reference Inc., World Almanac Books, Mahwah, New Jersey 1999, page 891.
[157] *The World Almanac and Book of Facts 2000*, Primedia Reference Inc., World Almanac Books, Mahwah, New Jersey 1999, page 891.

technological advances and the changing awareness of mass media. In addition, today, many societies require the acceptance of people with disabilities who often prove themselves beyond the most optimistic expectations.

Review of social ethics: At the same time and with relatively few problems, all people are acceptable in the workplace and are legally protected regardless of religious belief, sexual orientation, ethnic roots, race or color. We must add the ranks of political and economic migrants who occupy positions in millions of foreign employment positions outside of their own environments, particularly in jobs the native workers no longer want to take.

Educational realities: In the last few years concepts have entered the daily life such as 'lifelong' education, distance learning, business conferences. This is a clear departure from habitual behaviors[158] and dogmatic predispositions that enslaved past generations. In our opinion one should be critical of potential unethical behaviors that confine freedom of expression and learning. The employee is no longer possible to produce if he or she is not in a system in which there is training to new technologies and new business requirements. Many companies are involved in business-university alliances in their efforts to constantly upgrade their educational standards and to meet novel needs. The training of the human resources is of wide proportions. The offer of knowledge from the company to the worker is not only due to business ethics but is also desirable by the employee. At a time when the information redoubles every six years, it is a social imperative.

Quality of life: The labor conditions in England during the industrial revolution, give us incredible images of an outdated era. The employees worked hard for many hours without recognition, without any civilized conditions of health insurance, pension rights, free choice, free education, with very low pay, often under very difficult circumstances. Quality of life was something that the feudal lords of the past were entitled to enjoy while the masses were subordinates to them and possessed very few rights to the enjoyment, quality of life, or property. As we saw in Chapter 1, the analysis on ethical egoism, known philosophers since the era of Epikouros until the 18th century, accepted these associated positions. The following insert, from the third issue of the first year that the *Fortune* (Magazine)

---

[158] Ann M. Graybiel and Kyle S. Smith, Good Habits, Bad Habits, *Scientific American,* June 2014, pages 22-27.

was published, 85 years ago, shows how one of the top executives of the American Embassy in Athens considered the needs of the domestic staff.

> "At present I am paying $110 monthly for a good chef, an English governess, butler, maid, a general yardman and a gardener (the employer's annual income was $ 17,000). The servants think nothing of working from seven in the morning until midnight and are delighted when a dinner party is given, because of the Continental custom of tipping on the part of the guests."
>
> *Fortune*, May 1930, page 96

But in the last hundred years there have been significant changes. Modern companies with well-coordinated corporate cultures have very different perceptions of their employees. Workplaces, procedures, health matters and labor safety conditions have certainly changed completely[159]. Workers 'choose' their companies as the companies choose their employees so that there is harmony with the philosophy and culture of cooperation, expectations, visions and requirements. The remuneration packages include elements unheard a few years ago. Flex-time, work four days, provisions for special cases and so many others that are now a reality.

The management departments responsible of human resources have multidimensional functions that lead to upgrading the quality of corporate life, such as human resources planning, analysis and job description, recruitment and selection, training and human resource development, total rewards package of workers, assessment work and all employment relationships. Modern companies are seeking to attract "talent" from around the world and attract them to not only offer incentives like the above but also to be alert and committed themselves to the varied needs of their employees by providing free meals and quality gyms, veterinary services for pets of their workers or educational benefits of a wide variety of interests.

The new "principles" of workers

Given the social trends that we saw previously, but also because of progress and social welfare provided after the industrial revolution era, in most countries the roles of workers have changed significantly from those of 1900. Then, even in developed countries, the employee had much less

---

[159] Nevertheless we should observe that the opposite is true, too! Even in developed western societies "unhealthy" work ethics can force employees to continue offering their services in the presence of infectious diseases, thus, potentially hurting coworkers and customers alike. See Editorial Board, An Unhealthy Work Ethic, *Scientific American,* March 2015, page 7.

say in corporate governance and often was used in systemic roles of subordination.

For example, the U.S. academia considered that the generation born between 1926-1945, known to many as the silent generation, influenced more by the patriotism of parents and were characterized by a tradition in the obedience to country, laws and faith.

In contrast, baby boomers, who are considered as those born between 1945 and 1964, follow new trends are decisive, take more personal debt, they do not "sacrifice" or restrict personal expectations and pleasure for the benefit of others, they are challenging the hierarchy and the moral foundations of organizations and tend to describe the ethical and religious bases as 'mixed' existing beliefs, thus avoiding the narrow dogmatism of specific philosophical orientations.

If we move forward to the baby busters generation or generation X, 1965-1981, in numbers they are significantly less than both the previous and the next generations, perhaps because of high debt of the previous generation and unstable labor market, we see that they are characterized by uncertainty, a need to establish close and friendly environment and the perception that they are witnesses of very rapidly changing times. The last generation, is often called generation Y, 1982-2003, evolving into the era of mass media, computers, mobile phones, the internet. People in this generation of very young and isolated in their rooms and far from the direct supervision of the family, uncritically accept standard stimuli of an informal global education, largely produced effortlessly by sources of high readability. Observe, dear reader, for people of all ages, the potential of dogmatic behaviors due to IT repercussions as well as its impact on business ethics culture.[160]

Should we foresee the possibility of ethical dilemmas concerning the work place when there are presently statements like?

- In the new world of work, unemployment is high yet skilled and talented people are in short supply.

- A global labor market will not make every individual in the world better off: there will be losers as well as winners.

---

[160] Prophesizing future trends, similar behaviors were pointed out in George Orwell classic book *1984,* Penguin Books 1954.

> - Finding the right people is hard enough; keeping them motivated once they are in the payroll is even harder.
>
> Matthew Bishop[161]

As we saw in the debate of information and knowledge, the knowledge and skills students and workers learn, help them to experience aspects of the technological era and to acquire a professional competence, but may not provide them the ability to feel, to smell, to taste everyday life. It is envisaged that this generation is ambitious and demanding. It is also expected, the generation Y requires substantial changes to the now existing corporate cultures[162].

If you look at these critical stages of the silent generation, baby boomers, baby busters, and generation Y, we find parallels in other societies. Inference about trends in "principles" of workers, include[163]:

* Need for a work environment that is characterized by safe and quality infrastructure,
* Need for transparent procedures,
* The need for recognition of achievements,
* The need for respect and dignity,
* Presence of pride for the agency that employs the worker,
* Availability of vocational and educational development,
* Presence "package includes a competitive benefits and value pay of received bonuses, and health insurance coverage, and a broad base of other benefits, from nurseries to stock options,
* Presence of technological and competitive upgrades,
* Participation in corporate matters,
* Ability to personal choices in topics ranging from working hours to business promotions,
* A new, largely global, social perception of "principles" from the convergence (or confusion) of different cultural, geographical and temporal multidimensional aspects of reality,
* Corporate awareness, work, happiness of the individual, given the social

---

[161] Special report: The Future of Jobs, *The Economist,* September 10, 2011, pages 3, 5 και 12.
[162] Joseph W. Weiss, *Business Ethics: A Stakeholder and Issues Management Approach,* 3rd Edition, Thomson-South-Western, Mason, Ohio 2003, pages 213 – 315.
[163] See also John Dunkelberg and Donald P. Robin, The Anatomy of Fraudulent Behavior, *Business Horizons,* November-December 1998, pages 77-82.

role of the modern enterprise, which is no longer anthropocentric,
* Impact of information technology and immediacy of data transferring.

Alignment principles mentioned above are liable to confusion and result of multiple influences. Examples:

* A grandfather who lost his leg in the war and talks about patriotism and supreme human value and personal dignity,
* A father who gives a series of arguments in favour of material well-being,
* A mother trying to shown herself through the social scene,
* Powerful media acting as prosecutors and judges,
* Friends at the university who ignore any personal dignity in order to participate in reality shows,
* Constant mass media bombardment of luxurious lifestyles of successful business tycoons, actors, super-athletes while there is a clear understanding of poverty and misery in the largest part of the planet,
* Rising consumption of global products, existence of a global citizen, in many cases we observe the substantial prevalence of so-called imperialism through culture, and many other characteristics of the modern era[164] .

However we also see that within this multidimensional reality operates an effective social system that encourages knowledge creation, proven philosophical and religious beliefs, traditional values, a positive attitude, constant upgrading of the mainstream and protection of Planet Earth.

And yet, it should be clear that the "talent" of the work force is what makes businesses thrive in the global arena by offering tangible goods and services in a way never before possible. This "talent" can be accessed anywhere. Especially in careers which can be off-shored and outsourced via technological means such as computers and the Internet. For instance, the Indian, Chinese and Russian worker competes for the same position with the local Australian, Brazilian or Canadian worker. Consider, therefore, the business ethics repercussions while crossing national borders and life-long implanted moral behaviors.

Moreover, observe that the 500 largest companies in the world are employing less than 1% of the world's population, indicative that they actively seek talented individuals to generate, in average, more than about

---

[164] See Thanopoulos (2006) op. cit., pages 140, 146 (36), 73, 83

$475,000 revenue per person employed[165]. The old models of selection no longer are valid. Corporations do not operate with rules of democracy; they operate with rules of meritocracy! Therefore, modern work patterns will attract desirable employees by offering appropriate conditions and benefits. The provision of significant work incentives is not merely compatible with the business ethics of our time. It is imperative viability and business development.

Workers' rights

It is worth noting that the rights of workers were developed only after human slavery stopped, which is about 100 years ago. To put the matter in a time dimension, it suffices to say that before about 300 years a slave was "sold" for about 20 kg glass beads[166].

Earlier we referred to the employee in the 21st century and trends in sight. Also that workers and employers have certain rights too to be acknowledged harmoniously and not to be the cause of conflict or necessary legal or union actions. Hence now which are these rights?

Generally, we categorize workers' rights in the following sections:
The right to equitable remuneration: Supply and demand are usually determining the "packages" of rewards which, as with any other product or service significantly differ in their benefits. Also, the "packages" are dependent on working conditions, location, company profile, industry characteristics, environment, legal status and several other factors. We must add that each package of rewards is very sensitive to ethical norms that expectations depend on intangibles. For example, between two candidates with similar technical skills the one who will probably be preferred is the one with more positive and creative thinking. In our example, the cast of mind is a feature that cannot be measured and assessed easily or accurately, and thus to be rewarded accordingly.

Working in a safe working environment in well-developed laws and appropriately acting companies, the safety of the worker is an established right, non-controversial. But here there is a wide range of variations. For example, a company presents a trade show of the new uniforms that allow workers to handle certain types of chemicals at a level of protection which was unheard of until now. Even though we accept that the cost is not a

---

[165] See *Fortune,* Global 500, European Edition, July 21, 2014, page F-10.
[166] Henrietta Marie, Last Voyage of the Slave Ship, *National Geographic*, August 2002, page 59.

factor to be discussed regarding the safety of our employees, the question remains whether and when to learn about new technology, whether it can be available everywhere and in any event, or if it is possible for our company to monitor all developments in the industry.

It is often a lack of knowledge of what is available on the market which prevents us to master the most appropriate expertise on the safety of the workers. In parallel one must also consider the cost of acquisition of these technologies, the cost of implementing these technologies to existing business infrastructure, worker training in new technologies, security, etc. Here we should acknowledge that it may be possible due to ignorance, or deliberately, that the company does not cover security requirements and thus creates a moral dilemma, and perhaps legal. Moreover, in this case is possible that the appropriate remuneration is not given for work involving occupational risks. Also it must be considered, in the case where the employee takes some work knowing that the company did not cover the conditions of safe labor environment, since there are no suitable alternatives.

It is expected that the working conditions and the existing occupational hazards vary the total remuneration package (it is possible that the total benefits package may also include additional insurance funds to cover specific cases of accidents, family coverage, etc.). Though as far as the risks a work task involves, at least, the employer must fully inform the employee on the hazards of working and provide training in appropriate ways to address them.

The right to quality enhanced environment: A large part of our lives is to work. Workers in dark areas showed signs of depression and workers in faceless places of work environments long lost the zeal to work. Instead, well-designed workplaces contribute to more efficient, creative and original achievements. Here again we must see that it is not a guaranteed right of workers working in an environment of enhanced quality, but on a better balance of corporate culture it is to the benefit of the corporation to provide positive and integrated working conditions[167].

The right to a job that offers personal satisfaction: So many books have been written on the issue of job satisfaction. Again, the determining factor is the corporate culture and informal social contract proposed to the

---

[167] Milton Moskowitz and Robert Levering, The 100 Best Companies to Work For, *Fortune,* March 15, 2015, pages 60-72.

employees. It is recommended, to illustrate the vivid side of the issue, to indulge in one of Scott Adams cartoons which include a host of administrative and management issues which are examples of issues to avoid[168].

The right to employment without discrimination based on age, sex, race, color, ethnicity, religion, personal perceptions: In 1964, the United States of America passed the Civil Rights Act. In 1972 the Law of Equal Employment Opportunity Act continued the previous settings and essentially adopted the worker's right to equal opportunities regardless of age, sex, race, color, ethnicity, religion or personal views. Particular care is taken in cases where we are dealing with "working relationships", "business needs", "job-related" and "business necessity" and within large companies. Similar laws are found, after many years in many other places.

For example, the European Community gave the directive "establishing a general framework for equal treatment in employment and occupation" in November 2000[169]. However, although the labor employment rights without discrimination based on age, sex, race, color, nationality, religion or personal views are guaranteed in law, the substance is an appropriate business conduct that requires the appropriate arrangements.

The right to legal case management of worker: A wide range of rights is under this subtitle, and reports on recruitment, labor standards, assessments, dismissal, failure to communicate personal data, communications of workers, and so on.

It should be noted that the electronic age has created an environment, and in many cases a business culture that hardly protects communications of workers which become more vulnerable to interference of employers[170].

Alongside them should be pointed out specifically the right to transparent procedures, the right to become union members and the right to know the

---

[168] The principle of Dilbert: The least efficient workers systematically promoted there where they will be allowed to do the least damage: Corporate administration. Scott Adams, *The Dilbert Principle*, Harper Business, New York 1996.
[169] See *Official Journal*, 2-12-2000, Directive 2000/78/EC of 27 November 2000.
[170] Kenneth A. Kovach, Sandra J. Conner, Tamar Livneh, Kevin M. Scallan and Roy S. Schwartz, Electronic Communication in the Workplace-Something's Got to Give, *Business Horizons*, July / August 2000, pages 59-64.

facts for which he is concerned, whether this effect is due to business mergers, or internal procedural, or personal safety issues.

Employers' rights

Of course the employer has specific expectations from the employee, such as:
* Provision of contractual obligations,
* Participation in the procedures and the company plans,
* Acting in a lawful and ethical manner,
* Be actively working on reported hours worked and perform the promised work as expected performance wise,
* Do not assume work contrary to the corporate obligations (conflict of interest),
* To safeguard corporate secrets,
* Respect the company's assets and expertise,
* To maintain good relations with colleagues, superiors and subordinates.

There are many other categories of rights-expectations of the employer by the employee. And here we are again on the principle of balance. There is still an informal social contract that requires mutual respect, joint targeting, and agreement in principle. So often, specific issues are not expressly spelled out but are hypothesized ... for example, that there is faith in corporate vision, and what is called employee loyalty to the company, and in turn that the company will ensure they take care of their employees with lifelong employment, a principle we have noticed that is popular in a fairly large proportion of companies in Japan.

The principle of the balance of rights and responsibilities of workers and employers

The word 'right' of the employee may rely on legal or ethical basis or on a basis which combines both concepts. From a legal point of view particular rights are considered regulated, although there is always an ambiguity that often is determined upon the boundaries and legal limits and procedures used.

Here comes the business code of ethics and the interpretation that the corporate culture is giving to this code. A teleological thinking company can avoid short term ethics, and suffice to labor security arrangements necessary by law minimum measures. Another company, with ethical thought, takes good care that any action must be compliant with strict security rules, which may lead to higher costs. So we see that the business ethics act expands beyond its legal requirements arising measures. Of course, one could observe that ethical actions arising beyond legal requirements probably lead to better retention of quality workers, which increases the long-term productivity and give more validity to the company.

Why then are companies from their founding and without legal or trade union pressures, do not seek to offer better quality work, transparent performance evaluations, etc., etc. The answer is the lack of "knowledge" of what is the best way forward. It is not necessary because the business owner was great to be able to understand and all the issues his company faces. The company needs good advisers for the vindication of long-term corporate goals. And for the company and the employee is a profit to have a harmonious relationship, which despite the continued and necessary business and social pressures and changes, employees are always given all the guaranteed rights arising from the acceptable to the employee corporate culture.

That is, we are witnesses of a balance of rights and responsibilities of both employee and employer, from the convergence of principles and is related to the competitive environment, socioeconomic conditions, technological realities and legal requirements. We would say that companies should treat this as a management principle of high importance. Disregard can result in problems and labor strife.

We emphasize that the question of balance of rights and responsibilities are global and largely governed by the accepted philosophical basis of various locations. For example, in Japan, where the principles of Confucianism dictate harmony relationships, what the Japanese say wa, actually speak again for a principle of balance which requires integrity, fair treatment and respect. We also stress that the principle of balance essentially refers to an informal social contract that is continuously renewed according to new structures and business checks and is linked with the concept of incentives such as different geographical and business defined[171].

---

[171] Incentives are based on beliefs. See *Justice Theory and Expectancy Theory*, pages 312-315, Creg L. Stewart and Kenneth G. Brown, *Human Resource Management: Linking Strategy to Practice*, John Wiley and Sons, Inc., Hoboken, NJ 2009.

CHAPTER 6

THE ENVIRONMENT, OUR HOME

What you will learn in this Chapter

In this chapter you will learn concepts that relate to environmental ethics and specifically...

- About human interventions which are destroying our environment.
- About kinds of environmental pollution.
- About preserving ecological balance and wealth-producing resources.
- About legal commands protecting the environment.
- About moral ecology and business deontology.

Introduction to Chapter 6

Following our previously described representation, to us business appears as a three legged stool: Customers, employees, owners! Any leg cut means that the stool falls. We have already addressed issues on customers and employees. The following Chapter 7 deals with the owners. The present one deals with where this stool is standing: The environment.

We inherited a very fragile planet whose history and powerful evolution we barely know. Its natural balances are possible to change because of social and business interventions, especially due to technological possibilities we acquired during the last 200 years.

Realizing the obligation to be able to deliver one equally beautiful world to the next generations, ecological sessions and international environmental legal frameworks intend to enact rules of human and business behavior which will allow to preserve the variety of species and wealth of our planet. This, to us, is an ethical responsibility for all business activities.

Respect planet Earth

We learn daily about a number of environmental interventions as well as for measures and organizations that are trying to stop harmful environmental acts or decrease the impact of such acts. Of course, there is a natural planetary change which is following the laws of billions of years of evolution. However, people, especially with the technology we acquired during the past 100 years, intervene by wars, business, or socially, with energies that accelerate this alteration with unforeseen consequences. We have possibilities that we didn't in 1900. In ten minutes we swept away Hiroshima and Nagasaki and we no longer lack the means to destroy our planet many times. Yes, we have now the power to destroy, hundreds of times, the surface or our paradise, our home! We need to be much more sensitive, more ethical, less greedy and less egoistic.

However, beyond military confrontations, which let's hope are controlled, there are also social and business interventions whose part is very important. For example, consumer behavior and industrial uses overload the greenhouse effect. Since the mid-1800s up to just before the end of the past century, the average planet temperature increased at half Celsius degree. However, since then, until 2040 is optimistically predicted to be increased 0.7 degrees and pessimistically up to 3 whole Celsius degrees.[172]

Protecting our humble existence on this planet has always been the central point of attention. For example[173]:

- People everywhere feel offense because of the environmental pollution. Subconsciously they feel we passed limits we shouldn't have. They want to clean the world, make it better and become the earth guardians for future generations. James Gustave Speth, President, World Resources Institute.
- The challenge is to ...start rebuilding a world which will be in an ecological and human balance. Jerome B. Wiesner, Honorary President, Massachusetts Institute of Technology.

Yet, in March 1989 Exxon Valdez crashed into Alaska's Prince William Sound and 10 billion gallons of oil were poured, causing one of the greatest ecological disasters. This accident's publicity sensitized a big part of this planet's residents that however, with acts or omissions, participate in other impressive ecological disasters. For example, per the American

---

[172] Samuel W. Matthews. Under the Sun: Is Our World Warming? *National Geographic*, October 1990, pages 66-98.

[173] In January 1988 National Geographic Society had a congress with topic, worldwide environmental consequences with participation of distinguishing people. See Gilbert M. Grosvenor, Will We Mend Our Earth? *National Geographic,* Volume 174 No.6, December 1988, pages 766-771.

Environmental Protection Agency (EPA), car mechanics spill 200 billion gallons used oil to sewers when they change car oil. That is 20 times more annually than the damage caused by Exxon Valdez![174] Then, on April 20, 2010, we witness the BP's Deep Horizon accident resulting not only to human loss and enormous environmental pollution, but to a phenomenal settlement in terms of business responsibility[175].

Furthermore, scientifically we are not in a position to predict all the future results from the throwing of industrial and consuming waste. In the vast (ex) Soviet Union there have been many such violations of which the results we see right now. The pictures are revealing. Eight children from two neighboring areas in Moscow were born without their left hand, while in other places there are cases with dermatitis, births with bodily or intellectual imperfections have been doubled, and many more[176]. In the USA where EPA plays important part in protecting the environment, it's been observed that in areas where there is high use of pesticides such as McFarland California, cancer appears significantly higher than the inter-American average rate[177].

Human acting is the cause of similar problems. However, it's not only the small businessman's fault that spills the used oils in the sewer or uses dangerous agricultural medicines. It's not only the fault of large business which with cold logic calculated the cost of possible environmental damage and imported in the pricing of its product, the possible legal compensation which owes to the social community, because of its actions. We all have the responsibility for the future of our planet and it is required to be an explicit and strictly followed international ecological-ethical policy which will be referred to every aspect of possible environmental scheming.

Thinking ecologically...

We should all undertake our responsibilities for the protection of the environment if we want to contribute to the sustainable development of planet Earth. If we don't act responsibly, in a few decades from now, there

---

[174] Source: Used Oil Pollution Outweighs Tanker Spills, Earth Almanac, *National Geographic*, March 1992, page 138.

[175] See Claims Administration Website for the Deepwater Horizon Economic & Property Damages Settlement, last visited 4-4-2015.

[176] Mike Edwards, Lethal Legacy: Pollution in the former U.S.S.R., *National Geographic*, August 1994, pages 70-98.

[177] John G. Mitchell, Our Polluted Runoff, *National Geographic*, February 1996, page 119.

will be clear consequences in life quality, climate, rise of water level, extinction of animal species, new diseases or transformation of earth to a desert[178]. International organizations such as World Wide Fund for Nature (WWF) or Greenpeace International[179] are leading very important efforts for our Earth's future. Simultaneously, we must see that a part of this planet's population is not willing to discuss the question of downgrading of natural environment in a realistic basis. Business methodologies impose different approaches, though an analysis of 70 research studies reached in the conclusion that companies that surpass environmentally, surpass financially as well[180].

Man's intervention to his environment is variable and it doesn't only concern its pollution. Examples of this intervention include the reprocess of the water table horizon, water waste, fires, plotting, illegal buildings, lack of green, trespassing forests and beaches, illegal fishery, wildlife sanctuaries destruction, resources waste, non-use of alternative energy sources, non-use of waste management and lots more. This is a question of philosophy and ethics at the personal, business and state levels. Let's examine some infection dimensions that we, temporary residents of this planet, especially after industrial revolution, deal with improvisation:

Water Pollution
True case: In an underdeveloped country, in an ideal place near the sea, at around 10 in the morning we walked where the map showed there was a river and a bridge. The picture was shocking...many, many chicken heads and legs and feathers, apparently some slaughterhouse's waste, which was close by, went downstream towards the sea. Certainly, there is no need to go to some underdeveloped exotic country to see waste, dead animals, garbage, fruits floating into the beautiful little port, which protected by breakwater, doesn't have continuously renewed water. However, someone could reply with the argument that most of the above waste could create a visual pollution but in the end most of them are organic and will be dissolved soon through natural chain conversion, into something else. Attention, don't hurry to accept organic waste arguments, such as cesspool, slaughterhouse, wood etc. In water, organic waste is consumed by bacteria

---

[178] For example see, Laurie Garrett, *The Coming Plague,* Penguin Books, London 1995; also, Tim Appenzeller, The Big Thaw, *National Geographic,* June 2007, pages 56-71.
[179] See their websites: wwf.org and greenpeace.org respectively.
[180] See a new millennium meta-research on this matter: Harvey Meyer, The Greening of Corporate America *Journal of Business Strategy*, January-February 2000 pages 38-43. Since then, significant more similar works have appeared.

which deprive water from oxygen, which in good time stops being suitable as a wetland.

If organic waste create problems in water quality, a major problem is created by compound chemicals and inorganic waste. Agricultural pesticides, mine sulfur, phosphor compounds of industrial waste, used oils and cadmium and zinc and many more industrial and consuming applications, which as they come into water horizon, pollute water with essential results, usually unknown and often irreversible.

However, we must not stop at this point, because we have to examine particularly contagious toxic factors and radioactive waste and more topics such as water for refrigeration, which when heated is no longer in position to preserve life, fishes and other organisms.

Air pollution
Air pollution is often obvious even visually. In the air, there is often smell but in general it is not so easy to be detected. We keep degrading our air quality in many ways. Here are some of them:

- Producing great quantities of coal dioxide speeds greenhouse effect and affects in planets temperature, fusion of glaciers, floods, species extinction and many more.
- Producing chemicals such as CFC increases "ozone's hole" in stratosphere, allowing higher levels of harmful solar radiation.
- Industrial toxic gases travel like clouds and in the end become the basis of acid rains with incalculable damages.

Air, water and ground pollution issue meets with human choices, most of which have economic motives. Many of them were considered very reasonable and suitable some twenty, thirty, fifty years ago, when suggestions about sustainable development of the planet were non-existent, the environment was not so overloaded and scientific knowledge was not so developed.

Currently the top 6 countries producers of CO2 are China, USA, Russia, India, Japan, and Germany according to data compiled by the Energy Information Agency (Department of Energy), which estimates carbon dioxide emissions from all sources of fossil fuel burning and consumption. http://www.ucsusa.org/global_warming/science_and_impacts/science/each -countrys-share-of-co2.html

However, past strict views of industrial countries, seem to start to reverse. Henceforth, we observe in governmental and industrial level that systematic moves for the reduction of environmental pollution causes, are being made. Furthermore, downgrading of life quality because of the air pollution is obvious with a small comparison of living in the center of a big city instead of living in a place far from our technological civilization, let's say on a mountain. It is vital to realize that reduction of air pollution should even contribute to human life expectancy increase.[181]

Dealing with any pollution has become an imperative obligation for governmental or non-governmental organizations which with best intentions, involve in the problem's solution. Sometimes the problem seems to be more complicated. For instance, a non-for-profit foundation, the Dutch Face Foundation, plants trees in a national forest in Uganda and sells the relevant credits to the air companies passengers. With the credits income, it plants more trees. Obviously, everybody wins: a better national forest is being made, the atmosphere is getting clearer, air passengers feel that they participate in the creation of a better environment. Yet however, native farmers around the national forest Elgon, believe they lose their land and do everything they can to stop their area's reforestation[182].

Energy
Coal dioxide's production, chemical production, industrial toxic air, any kind of waste and so many more already mentioned, are associated with our planet's industrialization and our effort to offer to many people material comforts. For industry and for covering billions of people daily needs, energy is required. The facility of excavating and using coal and

---

[181] Typical similar reporting can be found at Velasquez, Manuel G., *Business Ethics: Concepts and Cases*, Fourth Edition, Prentice Hall, Upper Saddle River, New Jersey, 1998 page 256. Again, mile stoning data for the new millennium, during the last thirty years, air pollution measures is believed to contribute saving annually, only in the U.S.A., 14,000 human lives.

[182] See Stephan Faris, The Other Side of Carbon Trading, *Fortune,* European Edition, September 3, 2007, pages 66-74. A plethora of organizations exist today with similar objectives. For example "Face the Future" is an independent organization with worldwide operations, claiming that "it is our aim to mitigate climate change. Our team of experts specializes in the identifying, developing and marketing of forest values and biodiversity. In our work we focus on innovation and sustainable development" (www.face-thefuture.com , last visited 4-4-2015).

moreover using oil, covered almost all of the planet's energy needs until World War II.

In 1953, with a decisive speech in the United Nations (Atoms for Peace), the American President Dwight Eisenhower, stated the challenge of a new era, where atomic energy would play a decisive part. On the contrary with other energy solutions, atomic factories will be very expensive as an investment but very cheap in operating. But cases such as Three Miles Island (1979 Pennsylvania) or Chernobyl (1986 Ukraine), made ecologists and politicians restate their thinking. The result was the improvement of energy factories specifications, which now had essential geopolitical importance, since their first materials came from friendly countries such as Australia or Canada. Possible dangers due to these factories and the use of their waste are still under discussion. The fact that they don't overload greenhouse effect so much is an advantage and the same thing happens also with wind, hydroelectric, geothermal or solar energy.[183]

In comparison with previous statistics, facts seem very optimistic. Even in the U.S.A, where there has always been love for cars of big consumption, it appears that it is high time to replace high energy cost vehicles with others, more respectful to the environment. Let's see the other side now. The sales of the international car industry more and more move to developing countries, where in 2015, 100 million households will be able to afford a car. What does this mean? These markets did not exist fifteen years ago. Private car was only for the very wealthy. All these vehicles in such high numbers, even so small cars, some of which will come out to market for less than 2,000 euros and each, will increase the demand and cost of gasoline, petroleum and crude oil. And yet they will add a lot to the production of carbon dioxide and the greenhouse effect.[184]

For the informed citizen of the 21st century, the above have been analyzed extensively. Creating alternative energy sources, helps reducing greenhouse effect, contributes to non-reversing planets balance and it's a billion dollar priority investment with very important economic profits for the businesses that benefit from these opportunities but also with many

---

[183] Nuclear dawn, *The Economist Technology Quarterly*, September 8, 2007, pages 20-22 and Nuclear power's new age, *The Economist*, September 8, 2007 , page 11.
[184] Source: Keith Naughton, Small. It's the new Big, Newsweek, February 25, 2008, pages 34-37. In May 1974 there is a *Fortune Magazine* advertisement from Fiat, pointing to its very small vehicle by the then standards, stressing that the "yesterday's symbol of status is today's symbol of excess" (pages 114-115).

thoughts concerning business ethics[185].

Ecologically thinking, companies, states and people should focus in the use of alternative energy sources, avoiding environment pollution etc. At the same time though, we must pay attention to people who in position to provide the know-how of alternative energy sources and to incorporate this in a full system of business ethics and governing. For example, one of the largest oil companies, claims to have already a series of achievements in alternative energy sources, that protects humans and their environment, it co-operates with country governments to provide as "pure" and low budget energy sources as possible.[186] Reading these efforts, no one can but admire and praise these good business practices, which are direct, sincere and reliable to our planet needs. On the other hand, it ought to be circumspect about the future, when non inspired leaders, in a technocracy time, when a small number of businesses possess the todays state superpower part, are possible to enforce monopolistic practices pressuring a weak and uneducated future citizen.

Contamination of soil
We must not stop in the air, water or energy. Let's take a moment and think about how our grandmothers went shopping. They used to take a bag with them, in which they placed paper bags of the greengrocer. They didn't take plastic bags from the supermarket which are very difficult to split in the environment. Let's think the rag-man's profession. He really recycles productive resources. We can see that in the poor African village, they don't throw away plastic containers, because they use them to transport liquids or storing other things. We can see that in the very poor neighborhood of a big Mexican city, citizens open their metal cans and use them instead of tiles for their houses. Surely, there are many other problems, but here we see cases of recycling, of energy-in materials which in another society would be considered as garbage.

Let's see an industry that forces its suppliers to pack their missions with materials to be used further on. This happened for the millions of 'T' cars,

---

[185] T. Boone Pickens, a tycoon at oil producing area, has invested 2 billion dollars at Mesa Power for the construction of the biggest wind park until today and has wasted tens of billion dollars of his own money, to convince the responsible or not, to choose similar priorities. In May (2008), a report by the American Department of Energy, suggested the wind parks construction in twenty years, will cover the 20% of the American needs in electric energy. It is calculated that this goal realization will require investments of about 1.2 trillion dollars. Turbine Time, *The Economist*, July 19, 2008, pages 45 – 46.
[186] The Shell Sustainability Report 2005, pages 13, 15, 17, 25, 31.

Ford was packing. On the contrary, let's examine the very expensive packing of a French perfume which will be thrown out when we consume the 15 cubic cm of its liquid. Business has to study the results of used materials and packages. Additionally, all of us must study the consequences of used materials, fertilizers, packages, toxic matters, waste and radioactive products, businesses produce. As a business, we have to realize and value everything we use, whether it's some radioactive isotope from a medical machine, or it is recycling of a university paper. The business is able to realize its actions consequences sooner than the legislator. It is not a cost-profit interrelation. It is not just an extra dilemma of every business's people in charge. It's an essential command of respecting the environment and mortgage for the future generations to leave a better world. It is business ethics in practice.

Business selections about environmental pollution and the type of used energy are decisive for the industry function and for everyday routine of the citizens as well. For example, a car can have hybrid engines, an airplane can move with bio-fuels, a house can cover a part of its needs with geothermal or solar energy. Often, because of ignorance or inconsistency we decide to bequeath to future generations, a planet mistreated, poorer in living species or wealth-producing sources existence conditions of high risk. Unfortunately, the international legal frame doesn't have the mechanisms to impose measures for the ecological planet balance maintenance.

Legal directives on environmental protection

Progressively, countries acquire conscience that they must legislate the few allowed limits of damaging the environment, from noise pollution to biologic weapons. These regulations vary as far as their essence is concerned but in effectiveness of sanction impositions as well. It depends on the power of lobbies, actions which in some counties are considered necessary and in other are completely missing, with the arguments that are based in the laws of offer, demand and economic profit. In general, we can say that *the existence of international conditions of environmental protection and international law, obligates single regulations* from Austria to Australia and from Belgium to Bulgaria, although strong countries, such as the USA or China, follow with their own will the commands of international community[187].

[187] For a short but also compact topic analysis, the study of Bills Emmott "classic" article is recommended, Our law, Your law (part of the Survey of America's world role), *The Economist*, June 29, 2002, pages 20-23.

In the USA and at a confederacy level, important efforts are being made for a clean, civilized, non-polluted environment with a series of laws like Air Quality Act (1967), National Environmental Policy Act (1969), Water Pollution Control Act (1972) etc. It must be pointed out, that the substantial USA contribution to the protection of the global environment is rather superficial, having rejected Kyoto's convention about the climate and continuing using anthrax for producing energy with factories of very old technology.[188] On the contrary, the European Union, has expressed and follows essential views in matters that concern the protection of the environment.

Towards ecological ethics

International organizations such as World Wide Fund for Nature (WWF) and Greenpeace[189], have significantly contributed to the protection of the environment. At the same time, thousands less known organizations and famous personalities, attempt similar aims. The fact is that even though there has been an important progress in ecological sensitivity of today's people, we are very far from the existence of a global ecological conscience. As once, it was difficult to explain to the orangutan hunters that these rare animals' palms were not intended to be ashtrays and these animals were valuable, that's why today it's difficult to convince state governments, that the extinction of some small animals sanctuary must prevent us, from building one more barrier or that is possible that experiments for medical reasons may bring about lots of pain to creatures which some super power placed them to share with us planet earth or that a tropical forest protection makes our life quality better.

It has been stated by Stephen Hawking that "in 2600, the earth population will be so numerous that people would only be able to stand next to each other and the consumption of electric energy will make Earth shine like burning iron."[190] . However, it appears that academics finally turned their attention to ecological ethics mainly by the end of the seventies[191]. Since

---

[188] Environmental enemy No.1, *The Economist*, July 6 2002, page 11.

[189] Information about WWF from the site www.wwf.org.uk and for Greenpeace at www.greenpeace.org.

[190] Hawking, Stephen, *The Universe in a Nutshell*, Bantam Press, London, England 2001, page 159.

[191] Examples of some of the then major contributions are: K.E. Goodpaster and K.M. Sayer, Editors, *Ethics and Problems of the 21st Century,* University of Notre Dame Press, Notre Dame, IN 1979; William T. Blackstone, The Search of an Environmental Ethic, in

then ecological studies have bloomed and major contributions appeared. The reader would observe that the "platform" of ecological ethics could be seen in perspectives like:

1. Prosperity and evolution of "human" and "non-human" life on Earth have value themselves. This value is independent from the usefulness of "non-human" life for "human" evolution.

2. Wealth and all types of life variety, contributes to the real value.

3. People have no right to restrain wealth and variety of every life type, only for satisfying human needs.

4. The blooming of "human" life and culture, requires collateral "human" population reduction. In parallel, the growth of "non-human", requires reduction of "non-human" population.

5. Today's human intervention to "non-human" world, is exaggerated and the situation keeps getting worse.

6. Politics has to change. These changes will affect economic, technical and ideological structures. The result will be sensationally different from what is now advocated.

7. Ideological change reflects mostly the appreciation of quality of life...not the accomplishment of higher life standards.

8. Whoever accepts the above thoughts as correct, owes to take part, directly or indirectly, in materialization of the needful changes.[192]

From the above, the conclusion is that man, by assigning his space of surviving and evolving with selfish and economic criteria, creates a disharmony of ecological balance and eliminates the evolution of the "non-human" part of planet Earth. So, if a corporation's shareholder, believes the above, it is his business's obligation to evolve with ecological way of thinking the business economy, beyond all that are assigned by law and international circumstances. However, it is doubtful if logic of the above ecological conscience can flow evenly in all manifestations of the modern business economy.

The horizon of business programming, is much shorter than the circle of

---

Tom Regan, Editor, *Matters of Life and Death*, Random House Inc., New York 1979; Mary Anglemyer, et al., *A Search of Environmental Ethics, An Initial Bibliography*, Smisthonian Institution Press, Washington DC 1980; Donald Scherer and Tomas Attig, Editors, *Ethics and the Environment*, Prentice Hall, Englewood Cliffs, NJ 1983; Bill Devall, *Simple in Means, Rich in Ends, Practicing Deep Ecology*, Peregrine Smith Books, Salt Lake City UT 1988.
[192] Op. Cit, Velasquez, page 271.

creation and natural change. Nevertheless, it is necessary for every business establishment to act in an environmentally responsible way. The extent of this responsibility must be stated by its owners and managers and be expressed in a trustworthy fashion at the code of its ethics and deontology.

Thirty or forty years ago, the above views were not so clear. Business and ethics were contradictory meanings and the consciously ecological practices in business were very rare and pointed at in scorn phenomena. Today, as far as business thinking is concerned, essential changes are to come. Furthermore, and given that that business has now the particularly essential part in life quality, the future positive effect in the environment, must be taken as a fact. Additionally, business will begin to have visions beyond ecological approaches and suggesting social solutions and new business models which will focus on man, its character and on his whole happiness at work.

We must also see, what will happen if we don't accept, as a social group- not only as a business, a pro-environmental way of thinking. For example, for certain social groups it might not be acceptable for a citizen to waste the little water that is left to water his lawn, or hundreds of liters of petroleum to hourly propel his yacht or to possess two summer cottages or a private helicopter. Observe the world-wide attitude changes towards a more simplified living. Perhaps, from another point of view, will the materialistic motive, that was the basis of the capitalist system, create the basis of a social revolution, where the "simplicity and self-actualized driven" individuals will resist the "selfish wealth owners" in an effort to preserve environmental balances of planet Earth by restating the socially accepted ethical norms? Might our globalized society that offers more benefits to more people than ever, lead to a reality of respect not only towards every human or non-human species but to re-evaluation of every act, every omission and every process? Following the same type of thinking, may we question that some of the ecological type of investments might not be in the long run so wise and efficient business opportunities, especially in times of recession?[193]

In the next Chapter we shall examine the third leg of the initially described

---

[193] *Fortune,* European Edition, November 17, 2008 on Green Power: The markets are in turmoil, but these ten green stocks look like good bets in the long run. Marc Gunther, Doing well by clearing the air, pages 39-41. Michael V. Copeland, Solar stocks for a rainy day, pages 43-46. Todd Woody, Trying to catch the wind, pages 48-49.

as business "stool" that it is based on customers (Chapter 4), employees (Chapter 5) and owners. Therefore, this Chapter presented aspects of where our stool is standing, in regards to the environment, "our home". From another perspective we should see that although business had and has a teleological objective, usually defined by its owners as a short-term yield on investment, always connected to risk perceived realities (Chapter 7), one should also see deontological perspectives.

Yes, to a great extent and following thousands of years of social evolution, the present business thinking is still teleological. So, here we restate the initial image of our "stool", having three legs and standing on the environment. Clearly, even a century ago, humans did not have the ability to significantly affect it. They did not have the mass appetite to build everywhere or the means of destruction, or to use nuclear energy or technology.

CHAPTER 7

FINANCE ISSUES AND THE CODE OF CORPORATE GOVERNANCE

What you will learn in this Chapter

In this chapter you will learn concepts that relate to the ethics of corporate financing and governance; specifically ...

- About the owners of capital and the stakeholders of an organization.
- About corporate governance.
- About parameters affecting corporate governance.
- About the impact of shareholders in corporate governance.
- About the "e" bureaucracy in modern corporate governance.
- About the need for transparency in corporate governance.
- About propositions for the preparation of codes of corporate governance.
- Why unreliability of corporate governance and issues of dispute are always present.
- Suggestions for a better corporate governance.

Introduction to Chapter 7

If we look at the balance sheet of any organization, we see that its funds come from two main sources: Funds from shareholders and funds from lending. Without these funds the company cannot purchase equipment, market its products, acquire working capital or operate the business. In many cases we see that outsiders are hired for managing these funds whose owners believe that professional managers may make them more productive than themselves.

On the one hand the shareholders hope that professional managers, as administrators of their company, can do a better job than themselves. On the other hand, institutions which provide the required capital rely on professional expertise often seeking fixed-income return on their investment but also guarantees of timely repayment of the invested funds. Both groups are aware that there is an investment risk. The general rule is that the risk increases according to the expectation of higher return on capital.

It is clear that the company has moral obligations to its shareholders and lenders regarding the proper management of the investments with which they have been entrusted. We see therefore that there is a delicate balance between the administrators of the company and its owners. The larger the company, the more are the shareholders. The smaller the company, both the owners and the shareholders are more involved in corporate governance. Nevertheless professional management may require moral compromises. For example, a professional manager of a large company decides to make available part of the profitability of the business to altruistic purposes. He understands that this is part of the modus vivendi of contemporary enterprising governance. So, acting in a pro-social manner he reduces the dividend income of the company's shareholders. Is this ethical or fair for the far from rich shareholder, who in her old age, relies on the dividends of her investment, to undergo a cataract surgery? There are of course issues of legal liability. However we are obliged to see the whole picture. There is a vision, there is an environment, there is corporate governance, and there are venture capitalists, employees, customers, priorities.

Those who have enjoyed the role of responsibility usually are entrusted with a role of responsibility. Those who simply love being in power, usually lose it says Malcolm Forbes[194]. Nevertheless, we believe that we are in the midst of a transitional era. The ruthless investor and the powerful banker were the creatures of a post-industrial condition that, through legal means, enforced human submissiveness to their ruling elite. They were (and in most cases still are) the modern pharaohs, dictators, rulers. We are witnessing, however, a new age of social responsibility and managerial self-actualization which, although morally still caters to the investor specific financial needs, it supports a more tolerant public attitude that prefers modest inflationary options than enforcing government (or lobbying) propelled mass discipline and habitual behaviors. Nowadays,

---

[194] Those who enjoy responsibility usually get it; those who merely like exercising authority usually lose it. Malcolm Forbes, Goodman, Ted, Editor, *The Forbes Book of Business Quotations,* Konemann, Cologne, Germany 1999, page 720.

often matters of corporate finance, governance and ethics are treated far from the reality of business. The daily momentum contains 'philosophical' conflicts between members of the boards, managing crises, overseeing organizational issues, studying merger issues, and more[195]. This chapter will not be another report on the ethics of business financing through borrowing funds - that is a topic of other specialized works. After a short introduction on finance ethics we shall focus on building the code of corporate governance.

The owners of capital and their ethics

Let's face it! Historically, the owners of the land and the capital were always self-serving! They were the Kings, the Emperors, the powerful, the leaders. They had the armies, the whips and lasses. They were the commanders of justice, employment and of their luxurious idiosyncrasy. They were the self-propelled fighters. They were the industry leaders and the creators of wealth. They understood human suffering and sacrifice and they capitalized on it: through armed forces, understanding of human submission, discipline, religion, law and education, which were the means of their power. They were the rulers of customary attitudes and ethics. They created their own wealth and imposed ethical behaviors to the masses.

Yes, until the industrial revolution, it is our opinion, that the powerful imposed laws and ethical behaviors to the masses -for their own benefit.

Yes, even by today's standards the owners of wealth will determine the expected financial yield in accordance to the potential risk of losing their investment. This has little to do with the philosophical sense of ethics or fairness, or, using Sir William David Ross *prima facie* positions[196], remedial actions, gratitude, charity, self-development or non-abusive predispositions.

Yes, today there exists sometimes latitude of ethical behavior from the part of the owners of the capital. However in most parts of our planet we still experience lots of the pre-industrial era practices with respect to the financial yield. So, where is the light for capital owners' ethical behavior?

[195] A very useful tool on these issues is the Harvard Business Review on *Corporate Governance*, Harvard Business School Press, Boston, MA 2000.
[196] Discussed in Chapter 1.

Is there a deontological perspective with respect to the investor? It seems that there is, allowing managerial investment options and a series of benefits for employees which benefit capital owners as tax deductions - much beyond the financial remuneration of the owners of the capital.

We shall, therefore, revisit all pertinent issues at the Epilogue of this book. At that point we address again both the teleological and deontological perspectives of the modern era business ethics in terms of capital ownership, environmental concerns, marketing practices and human resource outlook. In our opinion, the industrial revolution brought a new societal focus away from the established rulers of the past and towards the everyday common man. Clearly the common man has gained a lot. Nevertheless, the commanders of wealth and of capital, as well as their immediate subordinates, from lobbyists to media-men and from government officials to persons of faith, are our epoch's new ruling elite which in our opinion venture their daily lives in two opposing directions: Some of them still live away from self-actualization mode, "employee happiness" and existentialist dimensions in secluded palaces, private jets, mega-yachts and superficial self-serving behaviors. The rest seems they understand that simplicity has to offer more than status quo, enjoying taking the bus, an un-ceremonial cup of tea, creativity or a heart-felt smile. We hope that we are witnessing a new era of social and business ethics that focuses on the individual citizen.

Corporate governance in the global village and the information age

The term corporate governance refers to the exercise of power (management) at the highest level of an organization or business, namely the board of directors. This is the hierarchical level which takes strategic decisions. Over the past fifty years, corporate governance faces spectacular challenges set out within the following parameters:

Internationalization

The global village offers new production opportunities, markets, investment choices, technological change, labor, administrative frameworks and tax heavens. It is very easy to move funds from one investment opportunity to another pursuing the most lucrative options, to make mergers, to utilize suitable information bases[197] and to analyze financial data reliably. This way the company's manager may invest its funds directly to the most lucrative international opportunities. By the same logic the global village allows business operations with minimal trade barriers. It should be noted that the global village gives the same opportunities to all. The competition is becoming fierce. The new competitor of a traditional Italian soft drink company is not necessary from Italy; it may come from Argentina, Belgium, or Canada.

Information and integrated enterprise resources

The phone, fax, the telegraph, the computer, the internet, the direct access to communications and databases provided managers business opportunities that did not exist before steam engines, supersonic aircraft, satellites or the electronic age. Within a few years each company could, if it desired to build its own website, allowing it to communicate with any part of the world, to accept orders and to process them to implementation, with virtually very few people involved in the process.

The management of this information has created a new administrative era which requires an electronic bureaucracy based on good quality information and sophisticated management systems, what we call integrated enterprise resource management and enterprise resource planning. The reader is advised to notice that changes of the existing enterprise resource planning system may not be an easy task and often individual managers, themselves victims of subconscious and habitual behaviors, are resistant to change, to propose and to implement changes of the technocratic bureaucracy they manage. In itself this has the potential of unethical repercussions, even of illegal ones, especially when confronted with cross-border transactions of financial interest.

Requiring transparency

The term transparency is new and is the new protagonist in corporate governance. Of course, somehow, the idea of transparency has always

---

[197] For example, any company can have access in Compustat, Business International, or National Trade Data Bank. Such databases are respectively sources of accounting data and information on business tips, and statistics. At the same time the reader should observe that we are in front of "A World without secrets"; most anyone can access information for personal or corporate purposes. See *Scientific American,* March 2015, Daniel C. Dennet and Deb Roay, Our Transparent future, pages 58-63.

been present but not always on the front stage. But it was present and known among the very few who had to know their business activities. Nowadays the business arena, must comply with the consistently renewed accepted accounting principles, prepared at the highest level of the company which must be publicly reported everywhere to all interested parties. Both the large institutional investors as well as the little old lady shareholder should know with certainty, consistency and transparency all the company data that the law provides.

As we said corporate governance is strategic management at the highest level of an organization. We would say, therefore, that corporate governance and its principles is something like the corporate "constitution" defining the responsibilities and relationships of all company stakeholders[198]. Let us therefore allow a regression of ideas. We believe it is necessary to have continuous feedback between the environment, corporate culture, organizational mission, corporate governance and code of business conduct and ethics. Therefore, and in order to successfully lead any organization, this corporate "constitution" must be continuously adaptive to merging and raiding propositions as well as transparent of its intentions and proposed practices.

The influence of shareholders in corporate governance

In legal terms the shareholders own and command the company and its corporate governance. However they are in the unique position where they have no legal responsibility for the activities of their company. They also have limited information and almost no power to take corporate decisions[199].

Moreover, they are the major influencers of changes that will affect the economic future of the company with grave ethical implications and ability to effect the new corporate order. Nevertheless, the majority of the people who trusted their money to the company will never understand what happened in the negotiations of the boards prior to reaching a new agreement, a merger of companies, a substantial new loan or a new

---

[198] The authors believe that only when all parties actively involved in the drafting of codes of business ethics and corporate governance principles, the harmonious development and the achievement of business and social objectives of the organization are possible.

[199] Anand, Sanjay, *Essentials of Corporate Governance*, John Wiley and Sons, Inc., Hoboken, New Jersey 2008, page 37.

issuance of stock for new equity. There is an important ethical responsibility for the proper management of those funds given by these anonymous third parties of investors who trusted the management team of the company.

One should also look at the corporate responsibility to others who have contributed funds to various corporate needs. Clearly, investors and bankers get a yield for their capital and take a relevant risk. In any case, the company must have an ethical behavior beyond a strict legal framework. The corporate managers' behavior must be true, have a social conscience and with knowledge must assess different markets and corresponding investment risks.

In summary we must emphasize that the shareholders are essentially responsible for the culture, the practices, ethics, and objectives of the corporation. As in our little town people have a responsibility for voting their future mayor, so corporate shareholders have a parallel responsibility. They need knowledge, faith in the corporate governance and effective participation, to exercise their democratic rights[200].

Unreliability of corporate governance and issues of dispute

In an era of globalization where information on corporate governance is easily obtainable, we are informed, almost daily, of cases of moderate or poor corporate governance[201]. Typical examples include: Acquisitions has proved shaky or questionable; sales of shares resulting to an impressive personal gain; business lobbying reversing plans and prohibiting auditing; accounting firms being business consultants to the companies which are their own audit business customers; controversial practices in the accounting audits of the company; charges of questionable accounting practices.

---

[200] For many, democracy in itself is, from an ethical perspective, a debatable issue. Is it for everyone? Can everyone exercise his rights? Under which conditions? Has the same rights someone who has been at the front of media, political life and education with a "marginal" citizen who, among others, spent twenty years in prison? From an ethical standpoint of view, what is better "democracy" or "meritocracy"?

[201] In our opinion one of the first attempts to highlight such events in a high circulation public medium was John A. Byrne, et al., How to Fix Corporate Governance, *BusinessWeek*, May 6, 2002, pages 44-50. See also next reference.

Joseph Neubauer, ex CEO Aramark Worldwide Corporation says that a whole life time is required to build a good (corporate) reputation and only a short time to destroy it. Therefore, they chose to accept the loss of time and money because they could not accept questionable trade practices[202].

The general areas that corporate governance has been accused of non-ethical practices are found in:

*Executive pay: It is usual presidents and general managers of companies to receive "packages" of pay in the tens of millions of dollars a year. The general feeling is that it is doubtful whether they all deserve it. At the same time, often it is questionable whether the leadership, which they inspired, was significant and substantial for the company they manage.

* Borrowing of stock issues: Persons in command are often remunerated in stock (corporate shares). Therefore, hey may place it a series of bank loans multiplying their amount, and since they have advanced knowledge of price peaks, they can sell for a maximum personal gain.

* The Board: The Board should have responsibility of the effective supervision of corporate affairs. There are many doubts whether the boards always act in the sole corporate interest.

* Accounting and analysts used: Disputes exist here as to the validity of the methods, transparency, and even detailed knowledge of those who take over accounting, auditing and business analysis.

* Regulatory factors: Companies follow the rules imposed on them by their environment. The mechanisms that regulate how businesses act sometimes have been too called into question. Business interests are very high. The corporate ability to transfer funds among tax heavens may result in less-than-ethical practices, independent monitoring systems and by-passing of the International Accounting Standards. In many cases third parties are allowed the capability to leverage a financial instrument of great monetary value without actually investing even a penny of their own personal capital funds.

---

[202] Explaining why they lost tens of millions of dollars in international contracts. Nanette Byrnes, et al, The Good CEO, *BusinessWeek*, September 23, 2002, pages 44-54. The article contains six profiles of "good» CEOs .

Suggestions for a better corporate governance[203]

Without effective corporate governance business efforts will yield lower results than the original business plan sought. It could be said that the lack of effective corporate governance is unethical because it wastes social resources. Therefore, un-meritocracy[204] in corporate governance is, in principle unethical. For example, there is no certainty that the son of the owner of the company is the best placed candidate to take over the governance of the large company that his father left him. Moreover, since antiquity, for the state government then, and for every government agency or organization today, when they are governed by unmeritorious, unworthy individuals, such actions have given rise to the grievance criticism and uprising of citizens[205].

Here are some suggestions:

Existence of a written code of corporate governance

States have laws and enforcement systems. The same applies for companies, some of them being larger, if we compare turnover of sales with a gross national product. The sound business practice is to have a written code of corporate governance which dictates the principles of conduct followed on which businesses and organizations rely to support their goals, procedures, and their actions regarding how they see their corporate social responsibility before the operation manuals are actually written. The code is written to be acceptable based on moral foundations, to have the capability of assessment of the business, allowing self-improvement of the business economy and to be guided by clarity, transparency, adaptability to continuously differentiating company checks and legal validity.

Take a hypothetical example of corporate governance: What would you do

---

[203] Two original collections of articles on corporate social responsibility and governance are: *Harvard Business Review on Corporate Governance*, Harvard Business School Press, Boston, MA 2000 and *Harvard Business Review on Corporate Responsibility*, Harvard Business School Press , Boston, MA 2003.

[204] Then what is meritocracy? Who can be an ethical and capable judge of the concept?
[205] A. Alexandridis translation of Epitaph Pericles ISBN: 978-618-80951-8-2 October 2013, schooltime.gr, Epitaph Pericles, page 24: ... υπηκόω κατάμεμψιν ως ούχ υπ' αξίων άρχεται.).

if you discover a great loss to your business[206]?

• Regarding the first move you should make: Gather as much information as you can; it will be useful. Bring your colleagues to help and you inform the top management. Do not gradually lose credibility by informing the public about more problems.

• Regarding how to deal with the crisis: Do not bring other external consultants. Act rapidly. Find out how to turn the problem into an opportunity to identify appropriate procedures to prevent it from happening in the future.

• With regard to responsibility: Do not deny responsibility. Do not charge others the liability. Do not criticize others.

• With regard to the practice of others found in the same position: How they addressed the issue and the administrative change. Learn to deal with crises (crisis management). Openness, truth and sincerity are the key resources.

Presentation of the company as a whole, administrative management flow, liability limits and need to revise the code of governance

Freedom is defined only within limits. In any system there are contact points where specific procedures are required to determine what is the way forward. In business the Governing Council (Board of Directors) acts as a representative of the shareholders and as intermediary between them and the Chief Executive Officer, the highest authority of the organization. The corporate structure must be presented with clarity so that all roles are clear and with minimal, if possible, duplication.

Particular attention is needed to estimate expected areas of future problems of the existing code of corporate governance, which may stem from the Board of Directors, the Chief Executive Officer, corporate finance, or even by their own shareholders. Here are some examples:

• Non-active members of the Board (or absence from) corporate achievements.
• Frequent rotation of Board members.
• Ignorance of issues from the Board, bad choice of members, problems in selecting members.
• Poor communication of the Board with investors.

---

[206] Bill George, Noel Tichy Jeffrey Sonnenfeld, respond on the issues. Note how their responses include the essence of moral and ethical behavior (Jia Lynn Yang, Lessons in Leadership: The Three-Minute Manager, *Fortune,* December 24, 2007, page 64.

• Conflicting interests (conflicts of interest) of members of the Board or of the CEO or key employees such as VPs.
• Communication problems and poor maintenance policy of the Board by the CEO.
• Poor monitoring performance of the CEO.
• Voting issues of shareholders (large abstention rate, minority achieves enforcement), and so on.

Address the details

In the business arena there are no "obvious" matters if they have not previously been clearly defined and understood. Something that is acceptable in Portugal may not be acceptable to Russia or Saudi Arabia. What could be acceptable by the corporate culture of ABB, it may not be acceptable by the culture of Boeing or the culture of Coca-Cola. Let's give some detailed examples of corporate governance that a corporate code should contain:

  • Roles, rights and obligations of shareholders.
  • How are the Board of Directors elected and the President of the company? What are their roles, obligations and rights?
  • How executives of the company are selected and what are their standards of work.
  • What is not permitted ..., e.g., relatives or questionable relationships to undertake specific corporate roles or projects.
  • What specific procedures and documents such as balance sheets, and so on should contain.

Systematic monitoring and control of operations

There is no existence of corporate governance without control mechanisms. In the formulation of corporate governance there should be a reference to the establishment of special committees. It is at the discretion of the company to decide which committees there will be. In our opinion, however, it is necessary to have a control and auditing committee. It should be noted that the audit of the audit committee in no way serves the role of an in-house 'Advocate'. The committee should direct the smooth development of corporate life and effective treatment of potential conflicts, reactions or mistakes.

We note that these proposals actually lead to more "bureaucratic", and possibly electronic bureaucratic, mechanisms. But the more internationalized the company grows, the more it needs to have a clear culture, a transparent and accountable corporate governance, and thus a consistently formulated social behavior.

Corporate social responsibility and code of corporate conduct

This is probably the most publicized case: On 31st December 1996 the stock of Enron was at $21,50. On 17th August 2000 it had reached $90. On 5th December 2001, the stock of the once 7th largest American company with turnover of 200 billion dollars was only $1.01. "Great ideas" of its directors for creating a company of low energy elements, which would keep a talented personnel but would try methods of the highest business risk, had tragically failed. Beliefs in ineffective and untested practices like "light-asset" strategies or "maintain a high credit rating and raise capital moving Enron's own assets off the balance sheet into complex partnerships" or "fostering a deal making culture" resulted in a great lesson of corporate social responsibility and code of corporate conduct as well as phenomenal human suffering and ethical issues.[207] The managers of Enron, not only were wrong ethically, but by their acts and omissions proved to be inferior to the circumstances. Remember the argument of a politician who speaks about political responsibility and taking political risk when his decisions have great cost for the anonymous crowd. Besides business ethics, there must coexist knowledge, modesty and judgement.

Modern business should sensitize in the way of thinking and rhythm of life of the social environment to which it applies and adjust its activities according to the generally acceptable principles of the area where it takes action. The contrary, that is the non-adjustment of business thinking, could create social reactions which would have as a consequence lower effectiveness, higher cost, market problems. We stand, consequently before a relatively new business practice where organizations consciously undertake social roles. This practice is known as corporate social responsibility (CSR).

Historically, this term, as well as the term social responsiveness, that is the corporate response to the social responsibility, appear as business practice

---

[207] The Fall of Enron, *BusinessWeek,* 17 December 2001, page 32. In addition, Sloan Alan, Lights Out for Enron, *Newsweek,* 10 December 2001, pages 48-49.

in books and in lots of articles about governing business since the decade of 1970. Among the pioneers, Peter Drucker introduced the term "social responsibility" as one of the eight areas[208] where the company needs to have objective tasks.

In lots of companies, there appears the issue of corporate consciousness, of the not-only profit tasks, the offer to employees, charity, ecologic thinking, protection of the weak of the planet and so many others. The unmerciful company of the industrial era, quite rapidly, realizes its social role, perhaps because this is to its interest. Its action flows more smoothly in society without facing reactions, and it sees better its opportunities.

However, labor syndicates, governments and state organizations indirectly accept their social insufficiency. They comprehend that they do not know and that they cannot successfully intervene in most cases where businesses, acting on their own benefit, are more effective. Businesses can find ways to upgrade its industrial environment or surgically intervene in a humanitarian action in a faraway land.

Traditionally, and as a reward, the only thing states can do is to recognize this effort, mainly adding a prize or a title of honor for the fame of the offering. Then, for the first time in 1999, at the world economic forum in Davos, corporate responsibility was presented as a social necessity and the Secretary General of the United Nations, Kofi Annan, asked big businesses to create a frame of reference of social responsibility, effectively presenting a human face to the world business. At the same time, the expression of business principles of the United Nations in November 1999, known as the Sullivan Principles, made the undersigned companies to accept[209] that they:

---

[208] Peter Drucker indicates that these eight areas are: marketing, innovation, human resources, organization, financial resources, productivity, social responsibility, profit requirements. See Drucker, Peter F. in *Management: Tasks, Responsibilities, Practices,* Harper and Row, New York 1974. Also, Carol Kennedy, *Guide to the Management Gurus*, Random House Business Books, London, England, 1989, page 54.

[209] *The Challenges of Corporate Social Responsibility*, The Philip Morris Institute, Brussels, Belgium 2000, page 9. The complete text, revisited at the respective website 4-4-2015, states about the "Global Sullivan Principles":
The Principles:

As a company which endorses the Global Sullivan Principles we will respect the law, and as a responsible member of society we will apply these Principles with integrity consistent with the legitimate role of business. We will develop and implement company

* Support economic, social and political justice everywhere and act as business.
* Protect human rights and encourage the application of equal rights.
* Educate and use employees at a disadvantage.
* Assist for greater tolerance and understanding among people, contributing to the increase of life quality of their business environment.

The code of corporate governance within the total business environment

In this section we shall study the code of corporate governance within the business environment. However, we must remind you, dear reader that before World War II, for most people, the term corporate ethics was an oxymoron statement. The two words could not coexist in the same sentence. Only recently, and mainly since the World War II, the societal role of business, and the necessity of its social behavior, has been clearly pronounced.

---

policies, procedures, training and internal reporting structures to ensure commitment to these principles throughout our organization. We believe the application of these Principles will achieve greater tolerance and better understanding among peoples, and advance the culture of peace.

Accordingly, we will:

1. Express our support for universal human rights and, particularly, those of our employees, the communities within which we operate, and parties with whom we do business.
2. Promote equal opportunity for our employees at all levels of the company with respect to issues such as color, race, gender, age, ethnicity or religious beliefs, and operate without unacceptable worker treatment such as the exploitation of children, physical punishment, female abuse, involuntary servitude, or other forms of abuse.
3. Respect our employees' voluntary freedom of association.
4. Compensate our employees to enable them to meet at least their basic needs and provide the opportunity to improve their skill and capability to raise their social and economic opportunities.
5. Provide a safe and healthy workplace; protect human health and the environment; and promote sustainable development.
6. Promote fair competition including respect for intellectual and other property rights, and not offer, pay or accept bribes.
7. Work with governments and communities in which we do business to improve the quality of life in those communities – their educational, cultural, economic and social well-being – and seek to provide training and opportunities for workers from disadvantaged backgrounds.
8. Promote the application of these principles by those with whom we do business.

We will be transparent in our implementation of these principles and provide information which demonstrates publicly our commitment to them.

The environment, natural-economic-technological-etc., affects us, as it affected our parents and grandparents and contributed to developing our culture. In parallel sense, the environment affects the creation of "corporate culture". And yet, as we saw in the 3rd Chapter, societies of the 21st century imposed business as a major social player, who had corporate culture, corporate philosophy and corporate ethics as well. The existence of general rules (codes) of corporate conduct has been already a fact and these rules were not a result of demands of social-economic environment of the last decades. Codes were formed after a more general reflection with reference to why and how business should act as far environment, clients, owners, employees are concerned.

Now see Diagram 7-1, from the environment to operation manuals. Corporate culture is subject to the environment business faces. So is the code of corporate ethics. Observe also that potentially business also affects its environment and all related matters. For instance, fifty years ago, people rarely talked about the greenhouse effect or the global warming. At that time most people did not consider them as important issues neither the meanings of corporate culture or business ethics.

Corporate culture sets goals (sales, profit, etc) thus defining the organizational mission which in turn becomes the basis for the code of corporate governance. As we said before the corporate governance document is parallel to a state's constitution. Consistent with the state's constitution are the laws, in effect the operation manuals of the particular business.

There is a continuous retroaction, a two-way relation, between corporate culture, ethics and organization mission. There is the same between corporate ethics and corporate governance. Only at the operational level, corporate ethics dictate the operation manuals and implementation processes.

Diagram 7 -1: From environment to operation manual

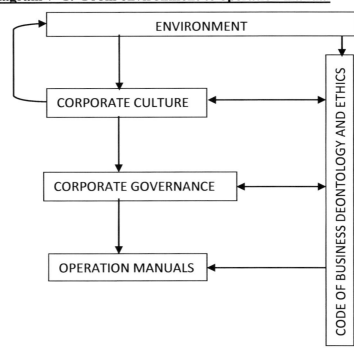

The contents of corporate governance … revisiting ethics

Perhaps in a philosophic discussion after dinner, some businessmen would find ideally correct to support economic, social and political justice, to protect human rights and encourage the implementation of equal rights, to educate and use deficient employees, or help in existing greater tolerance and understanding among people, thus contributing to better life quality of their business environment. In private, however, we can understand this, most of businessmen themselves would say to the polite coordinator of such a conversation…." what are you telling us right now?" The business is meant to make money, not to do social work. We are not interested in equal rights, we do not want to use people with natural imperfections, and so on". What could our answer be?

Perhaps the polite coordinator of the pervious conversation would himself have his doubts. Is it possible that there is only one approach that every social system could accept as true? In the first chapter, we saw that there are different opinions relating to the era, the principles, the philosophical approaches, education, economic needs and lots more factors.   By the same token, could somebody see the world in the same way the others see it? Or could an employee face corporate issues in the same way of thinking with his colleague? Or could a business see "an industrial patent" from the same of view another business sees it? Or could a valid institution always have the know-how to be able to foresee the results of its decisions?

Let's see some examples:

- Somebody stops at the red light and takes advantage of waiting to empty the ashtray of his car onto the road. Someone else always brings a little bag with him to collect his rubbish.
- A newly rich wastes a lot of barrels of fresh water to fill his swimming-pool which stands only for decoration and not for swimming. In the same prefecture somebody else, deprives himself of his poor pension, to buy bottles of drinking water which he gives anonymously to the people of the nearby village suffering from a devastating fire.
- A veterinary doctor makes experiments to little monkeys and in the name of science makes them suffer and die. Someone else supervises the quality of dairy products and is a vegetarian.
- Due to economic profit, a doctor suggests an urgent surgical operation while someone else follows a many-month painful for him conservative treatment.
- A business thinks that it needs a leading-edge research to be strengthened, while another one, in the same field, waits to take advantage of others' industrial patents, when these have been abandoned by the previous ones.
- Within the bounds of his paid work, a researcher finds out something important which the business patents and earns billions euros from it. According to his contract, the researcher has no other benefit from these except for his salary. Unfortunately, when the researcher has retired from his job, his only child needs $250,000 for medical expenses. The company does not admit any moral obligation and so the father sells his house for his child's medical care.
- In a similar case, a creative painter composes a fantastic comic hero, and being poor, sells the copyright for him, for a small sum of money. This hero meets world success but none helps the suffering creator any more.
- The business of Mr. X employs hundreds of employees to whom it offers perfect working conditions. Moreover, the company has one of the most advanced codes of corporate governance and is considered

to be a model of ecologically thinking and social responsibility. However, during weekends, Mr. X likes traveling to the Aegean Sea on his private yacht of twelve million euros, consuming over 200 liters of petrol per hour and great amounts on social events and personal security guards. Couldn't all these be considered contradictory to his corporate way of thinking and waste of social resources?

- In the first explosions of atomic bombs in the Atoll of the Pacific Ocean, those who witnessed the explosions, not knowing, took only the most necessary measures of protection. One may wonder if today the production companies are aware of the results of modified products, biogenetics, bio-electronic medicine or mobile phones?

- Why it isn't possible, men from Athens, no, it isn't possible, for someone to gain stable power based on injustice, perjury and lies. Demosthenes[210].
- I believe, Socrates that the conscientious differs from the greedy of gain in this: The first one is ready to get tired for praise and honor, to expose himself to dangers and be held back from profiteering. Xenophon[211]
- To be somebody important, one must have virtues. To act someone correctly in politics and by extension in business, one must be of great morals. Aristotle[212]

A business deontology code, the springboard of corporate governance principles, has to be composed by people whose thinking at least coincides with that of the company's owners. Obviously, their thinking and resulting principles can differ among companies according to the object, place, knowledge, intentions and lots other relevant factors.

From the previous discussion, it is clear that it is especially laborious for the business ethics code to be composed, which as we have aforementioned, will be the base of the code of its corporate governance and precedes it. Given that the code of corporate governance of each organization is mainly "its constitution", that is the utmost text of defining obligations, commitments, relations and processes, before composing this code, therefore before the composition of the basic points of business

---

[210] Demosthenes speech, *Olynhthiakoi B*, Editions Papyros, Athens, Section 10, page 278.
[211] Xenophon, *Economic- Resourses,* Editions Cactus 127, Athens, March 1993, Section 10, page 148.
[212] Aristotle, *Ethics*, Great A, Editions Cactus, Athens 1992, Section 25, page 50.

ethics, there is required the acceptance of bounds according to which these codes can be developed. The following pieces of advice allow us to express more completely these bounds:

Practical use: Such a code is being made so that the company, sensitized in the needs of the region it serves, it aims to be able to maximize its business benefits by being a better and more responsible citizen.

Business processes: There must be clear processes which will give the possibility of evaluating the efficiency of the results of this code, which additionally must be transparent and trustworthy. Be not involved in private tug-of-wars, no matter how important they may be. In business everything must be solved only by processes.

Control and penalization: This code is applied prudently and respectfully to all stakeholders; that means whoever it applies to, should check if the outlined principles have been kept and to set penalties if there have been any infringements. There must be also the means for these regulations, in the highest corporate level possible.

Perennial dimensions: This code must have adaptation flexibility in a continuous base. It must be able to predetermine the future of business. It should be supervised by people of social experience and vision.

Perception of environmental situations and differentiations: The company takes action in different environments, with special social, cultural, economic realities. Such a code must be extensive enough to include these differences, to have the possibility of adaptation in environmental changes.

Correct preparation and creation of business plan with appropriate time limits: Avoid forced movements. Collect the necessary information from all stakeholders. Define the area of ethics concerned and study it. Find who and what it concerns. Which can the legal complications be? Which are the moral and social results if there is or if there is not some reaction? How do the others inside and outside the company perceive it? Think positively, but for the time being, do not enter into details. In essence, the development of a corporate governance code should require to follow all steps of a business plan.

All participants of the business, from employees to clients, must "be listened to" if such a code is to be composed. If such an effort is to succeed, there should have been previously approved, at every administrative level, a plan, the economic means and relevant schedules. Lots of working hours are to be demanded and business priorities will be conflicted because executives should be used far from their operational commitments.

Conscious self-control: Armed with the rough plan mentioned above, think of the others' reactions. Ask your director, what he thinks of your thoughts. Think of your family. Would they agree with this initiative of yours and the consequences of your actions? Think of your idea and your method to be made known by the media? Would perhaps be any problems due to this presentation or/and a possible distortion by the media? What would you do then? Before moving on, calm down, wait for a little, and think of it again. Perhaps there is something similar in your business. A relevant fact may be pre-existed. Consider that.

Based on the principles of Caux Round Table....

To compose a code of business deontology, it is necessary to revisit how this idea started and what it should contain. Since 1986, a group of business executives in Caux-sur-Montreaux in Switzerland, made the first formal expressions on issues of business ethics. Later (1994), based on the principles of Minnesota Center for Corporate Responsibility (1992) and believing that businesses have the possibility to upgrade all peoples' life quality, expressed a series of views known as the Caux (Round Table) Principles. These principles based on two hubs: On human dignity and Japanese kyosei, which can be translated as living and working together for the common good, enabling cooperation and mutual prosperity to coexist with healthy and fair competition[213].

---

[213] Laura P. Hartman, *Perspectives in Business Ethics,* Second Edition, McGraw-Hill Irwin, New York 2002, pages 737-740. also see Joe Skelly, The Caux Round Table: Principles for Business, The Rise of International Ethics, *Business Ethics*, March-April 1995, pages 2-5 supplement. Also see how the term is used in the codes of corporate governing of large international companies. For instance, Canon (in its official website, February 22, 2015) indicates that "*Kyosei* also drives our commitment to establishing good relations, not only with our customers but also with the communities in which we operate." The meaning of kyosei refers to all people, regardless of race, religion, or culture, harmoniously living and working together into the future.

But how these principles are seen today? Using as platform statements from Conscious Capitalism Inc., the following four issues are defining a new era:

1. A purpose other than making money, though the money should make money, too.
2. A focus on employees, customers, suppliers, the community and its ecosystem-and its shareholders.
3. A leader who seeks to bring out the best in people.
4. A culture that fosters love and trust[214].

The basic expression of these principles may be formed in three stages: a) introduction, b) general principles (responsibility of business to its stakeholders, economic and social responsibility of business for innovation, justice, fair offer to the world community, business responsibility beyond the letter of the law, concept of trust, respect to processes, defense of world trade, respect to the environment, and avoidance of illegal actions), and (c) principles for participants (clients, employees, owners, suppliers, competitors, and local societies).

Following our previous discussion of the principles of Caux Round Table we tend to suggest that a code of corporate governance does not express detailed actions such as:

- Offer of voluntary work for preserving the environment,
- Financing of scholarships for persons with special needs,
- Payment of the company's human labor in a level above the average of the branch.

By the same token examples of general statements that can be found in such a code could be the following:

- Respect for the environment, its defense, avoidance of any waste.
- Avoidance, or silent acceptance of illegal actions, such as money laundering or improper actions,
- Actions based not only on the letter of the law but on its substance and the unwritten customary admissions,
- Production and trade of products, producing social interest of every special market where business takes action.

---

[214] Susan Berfield, The Clutter In Kip Tindell. *Bloomberg Businessweek* (special Issue focusing on Profits vs. Virtue), pages 40-45, February 23-March 1, 2015.

Previously we studied particular aspects of business behavior as far as customers, employees, owners, the environment in general are concerned. There are being quoted now, summarizing previous examples of rules or principles to every group of people depending on the company, of stakeholders, which could be included in the code of a corporate governance:

To customers:
- Provision of the highest quality products,
- Possibility of every complaint to be confronted,
- Attention to the safety of products.

To employees:
- Contemporary, safe and sanitary installations,
- Satisfactory salaries and work conditions,
- Fair work assessment in transparent ways,
- Equal possibility of hiring, independently of sex, age, religion or origin.

To owners:
- Informing with transparency and credibility,
- Application of correct management so that there will be good management of the money trusted,
- Offer of competitive benefits.

To suppliers:
- Application of moral values,
- Fairness and justice of processes,
- Observing that they follow the corporate ethics principles,
- Selection of their own suppliers in accordance to the established corporate principles.

To the social environment:
- Respect to the peculiarities of every local culture,
- Offer, where it applies, social work and money support for beneficial efforts,
- Business deontology respecting institutions and defending laws.

To competitors:
- Promotion of business thinking of free competition, without using morally doubtful means,
- Promotion of socially accepted methods of competition and competitors' respect.

The above mentioned are examples of what a corporate governance code can consist of, or as it is otherwise said, code of corporate social responsibility. We have to point out here, that this definition is still unstable. The conception of the term *corporate social responsibility*, varies from university to university and from country to country[215]. At the same time, this code must offer business the possibility to adjust or better to sensitize according to local realities. Some people, for example, will indicate that the parent company should avoid to refer to its own system of values. For instance, let's assume that a Canadian company decrees that employment of the minor is not allowed. What will happen if in a small town in India, where a supplier has the production factory, the minor workers, due to local reasons, are the only ones who can work and support their family?

> - Many companies do nothing with their ethics codes. They simply hang them somewhere on the wall to be seen.
> - Many activities are neither good, nor bad, but they exist in the morally free space.
> - If a company said that any gift is immoral, it could not operate in Japan[216].

Towards a code of corporate governance: Summarizing ....

Reading this book, it must have become clear that the code of corporate governance is a part of a total organizational design. This design starts from corporate culture, moves on to research and consciousness of the business environment, revisits the corporate principles and the bounds of social corporate responsibility and ends with a document of corporate governance.

Observe that "good practice" does not prove the existence of any code or the essential corporate social responsibility. Often a "good practice" appears to be a correct social action, but a deeper study brings us to the conclusion of a superficial approach of corporate social responsibility which is done only for making impression in the areas of public relations, marketing or human resource management.

---

[215] Sarah Murray, Corporate Social responsibility: Now is the time to clarify the true meaning, *Financial Times*, January 21, 2002, Supplement on business education, page 10.

[216] Thomas Donaldson, Values in Tension: Ethics away from Home, *Harvard Business Review*, September-October 1996, pages 48-62. It is interesting that although this was written twenty years ago, it is still valid today.

If your organization is truly committed to implement it, this is probably a clear indication that the organization aims to see itself as an institutional player with a grave societal role. Do not forget that such organizations directly want to tell their stakeholders that they aim to assist them to "reach their full potential!" And, if the company management wants *you* to undertake the task of delivering this code, you must be sensitized to the issues discussed at the previous two subchapters, but also on:

The support of top management: If the Board of Directors, Chairperson, CEO, and anyone else who decides about the future of the company, is not 100% behind the idea of a code of corporate governance, do not labor in vain. Remember that corporate governance includes statements about all corporate stakeholders and touches on their personal sense of philosophy and ethics. If the top management is not behind you, such document can be written, but its implementation will be very difficult and may be superficial.

Existence of previous corporate experience: All stakeholders are involved in this process. However, they must provide inputs following standardized processes. Otherwise summing up their inputs will be of debatable value, it will be untested and of questionable value. Therefore, previous corporate experience with ISOs, ERPs, vision sessions, sensitivity training, etc., will be very useful. Capitalize on advisors and prepare for a meaningful educational effort.

Have in mind that specialized assurance standards exist that may lead your thinking in targeted approaches varying from environmental to labor practices. Such standards are the ISO14001, the model of social responsibility SA8000 (Social Accountability 8000), or the AA1000 Assurance Standard, which started in 1999 from the Institute of Social and Ethical Accounting. We advise to familiarize yourself with them before you start[217]. Finally, allow us to repeat that an organization's code of ethics and its subsequent corporate governance documents demands participation of all representative departments and all stakeholders.

---

[217] See www.iso.org, www.accountability21.net, www.accountability.org , www.sa-intl.org .

Epilogue: Living Together

Our era has been characterized by the existence of business, a cultural phenomenon that wise men and writers of the past had only superficially valued. It has imposed behavior norms, educational models, research rules, developmental approaches which will very soon allow every human being of this planet to enjoy a comfortable way of living. However, business itself has evolved so fast, that its philosophy as well as its processes of operating, auditing and total behavior are not as yet firmly grounded, in order to guarantee that its mechanism will not dictatorially rule the planet but will specify principles of spiritual evolution and emotional balance in a peaceful world.

In this work, we studied basic philosophical issues affecting ethics, such as deontology or teleology. We also studied aspects of our times, such as our globalized village, the demise of the family, the incredible technological evolution and the usage of a spectacular amount of information. In the process we aimed towards a better understanding of the corporate world, pointing to some of its "ethical" faults and the need to express a code of business ethics and deontology in every organization.

It would be technically easy for these new principles of business ethics to be created and the future business models to be socially sensitized. In fact, this is the reason that led to this book's script--to further promote the creation business ethics codes and the respective corporate governance tooling.

The thing that concerns us most is the lack in today's human character. In our opinion, today's man doesn't react, falls into fixed social patterns, doesn't search, doesn't revolt and doesn't change. Technology imposed to him projects an enslaved social behavior, the hours that he will spend in front of his television and computer, his bodiless occupations and enjoyments, the limits of studying, development, social evolution, offering collaboration. He is a happy, impersonal, representative of a materialistic reality that teaches him what a purpose, enjoyment, future is. Constantly changing social intuitions create "group thinking". The virtual reality, doesn't capitalize on the individual sensitivities. Rarely one finds reason for in-depth analysis, critical thinking or self-actualization.

So, unfortunately, social patterns bring the today's humans very close to what we see as a medieval reality mainly propelled through culturally standardized and technically supported means, a reality which confines human thinking, hope and spiritual quest.

Knowing that our planet's population soon will surpass the ten billion mark, a worldwide effort must be undertaken towards a speedy upgrading of the social being. A worldwide effort (where leaders will be wise capitalists-modern business leaders) with common purpose to redistribute means, health, education, progress, human happiness and personal credit, in an environment that will guarantee evolution stability and viability and evolution of all the living beings of planet Earth. Arrogant, selfish and mostly materialistic demands or social resources' blatant waste should not be allowed. Observe that it has been argued that humans "conquered the planet" using as their "ultimate weapon: cooperation."[218] This requires personal philosophy, entrepreneurial thinking, ethical behavior and self-actualization potential. Otherwise, a danger for a different type of worldwide social revolution is to come. But this topic will be another writing target.

For now, we must try to materialize goals of corporate social responsibility, business philosophy, culture, ethics and of corporate governance. These goals, develop differently for each business, but apply to every governmental or non-governmental organization. These goals' development, depend on the needs of time, peoples' maturity and local legal frames. In general though, we should repeat our statement in the very start of this book: These goals must have a teleological character, which will define the footpath that will be achieved. This difficult path is being defined by deontological decisions, regarding employees, clients, owners and environment in general. Moreover, we could say that because the business plays the particular important part in the quality of life, its

---

[218] Curtis W. Marean, The Most Invasive Species of All, *Scientific American,* August 2015, pages 22-29.

influence in the environment must be considered from a point of view that envisages beyond ecological approaches and suggests social solutions.

And, for a moment and once more, let's reexamine the global legal frameworks that rule differently on similar cases as we are moving from one country to another. Let's question who qualifies to tell us what is legal for the society we live in, and why? What about the legal usage of software enabling universally anonymous communication? Do we change our perspectives in our challenging new era that combines globalization, legal compliance, personal philosophies, ethics and advance information technology desiderata?

The above thoughts have specific importance, especially at a time of worldwide recession, like the one we are now experiencing. This recession, is coming from indigence, from working laziness, from non-professional actions, from easy drifting temper, from social web's insubstantiality, from the lack of leadership, principles, goals. In fact, this recession is a derivative of an inflationary thinking and practice in economic and social fields. It is also the moment of catharsis. That is the time for new opportunities. It is then, that we see that we discriminated, when we moved slowly, how the mistakes were made.

So, we come to this era's driving force which as we said in this work, is not other than business organizations. And, since today all business is global, if our globalized business realizes not only its economical reason of existence, if it precedes the philosophy and ethics and if it composes the code of corporate governance with caution and flexibility, people may then avoid future economic and social crises and live in an environmentally friendly world, peacefully together!.

So, the burden falls to the wise leaders of modern business, to their mentality, their education, the evaluation of their projects, their choices.

As we conclude our Business Ethics text we promise you, dear reader, that we aim to have soon a Business Ethics Practice text. Why? Because all around the world business ethics practices are very different and depend on cultural specificities, individual upbringing, societal fabric and corporate decision making. So, allow us to briefly present a couple of examples from this next text:

Case one taken from Bloomberg Businessweek, The New Money Issue, meet the rising class of global hustlers (October 11, 2015). : Have you heard of feudal China'a second generation rich kids, by some that "they know only to show off their wealth but do not know how to create wealth" (ibid., page 58)? Imagine that "the son of China's richest man posted photos of his dog wearing two gold Apple Watches, one on each forepaw (ibid., page 55).

Case two, taken from Fortune September 1st 2015 issue #11, pages 16-32: It starts with a short article from Alan Murray, Doing Well by Doing Good and continues with a list and case examples of fifty such companies. We agree! The future of capitalism-and the future of mankind-depends on companies that are making genuine efforts to change the world for the better (ibid., page 17).

References

(In) Search of the good company, *The Economist*, September 8, 2007, pages 61-62.

(The) Challenges of Corporate Social Responsibility, 2000. Brussels, Belgium: The Philip Morris Institute.

(The) Economist (Pocket) World in Figures, 2001 Edition, The Economist in Association with Profile Books Ltd, London, UK 2000.

(The) Economist (Pocket) World in Figures, 2008 Edition, The Economist in Association with Profile Books Ltd, London, UK 2007.

(The) Economist, Special report on business and climate change, June 2nd, 2007.

(The) Global environment (survey), The Economist, July 6th, 2002.

(The) Shell Sustainability Report 2005, pages 13, 15, 17, 25, 31.

(The) Urantia Book, Urantia Foundation, Chicago, Il 1955.

(The) World Almanac and Book of Facts 2000, Primedia Reference Inc., World Almanac Books, Mahwah, New Jersey 1999.

AACSB Task Force 2011. Globalization of Management Education: Changing International Structures, Adaptive Strategies, and the Impact of Institutions. Bingley, UK: Emerald.

Abdi, M. & Aulakh, P. S. 2012. Do country-level institutional frameworks and interim governance arrangements substitute or complement in international business relationships? *Journal of International Business Studies*, 43(5): 477-497.

Accessed 20/06/2011.

Adams, Scott, *The Dilbert Principle*, Harper Business, New York 1996.

Adler, N. J., and Bartholomew, S.1992. Academic and Professional Communities of Discourse: Generating Knowledge on Transnational Human Resource Management, Journal of International Business Studies 23(3):551-570.

Albrecht, William P., *Economics*, 2nd Edition, Prentice-Hall Inc., Englewood Cliffs, New Jersey, 1979.

America's largest corporations 2002: The top 500, *Fortune*, (European Edition), April 22, 2002.

Anand, Sanjay, *Essentials of Corporate Governance*, John Wiley and Sons , Inc., Hoboken, New Jersey 2008.

Anglemyer, M. et al. 1980. *A Search of Environmental Ethics, An Initial Bibliography.* Washington, DC: Smisthonian Institution Press.

Anglemyer, Mary et al., *A Search of Environmental Ethics, An Initial Bibliography*, Smithsonian Institution Press, Washington DC 1980.

Apostle Paul's letter to Romans, chapter B, lines 14-16.

Appenzeller, Tim, The Big Thaw, *National Geographic*, June 2007, pages 56-71.

Aristotle, *Ethical Greatness A*, Editions Cactus, Athens 1992.

Arthur Andersen LLP Facts, Available on line at: http://www.jiffynotes.com/a_study_guides/book_notes/cps_01/cps_01_00033.html . Accessed 20/06/2011.

Athanasopoulos Konstantinos G., The Ethical Nature and the Person's Freedom. Tipothito,Giorgos Dardanos, Athens 2002.

Aulakh, P. S., Jiang, & M. S.. Pan Y. 2010. International technology licensing: Monopoly, rents, transaction costs and exclusive rights. *Journal of International Business Studies*, 41(4): 587-605.

Babiniotis Georgios, Greek language dictionary, Centre of lexicology, Athens 1998.

Bahree, Bhushan, Carlta Vizthum, and Erik Portanger, How Hard Lessons of the Past Sealed A Tanker's Fate, The Wall Street Journal, November 26, 2002, pages 1 and 12.

Bainbridge, Stephen M., The Complete Guide to Sarbanes-Oxley, Adams Business, Avon Massachusetts 2007.

Beauchamp, T. L. & Bowie, N. E. 1997. *Ethical Theory in Business*, 5th Edition. Upper Saddle River, NJ: Prentice Hall.

Beauchamp, Tom L., Norman E. Bowie, and Denis G. Arnold, Ethical Theory in Business, 8th International Edition, Pearson Education, Inc., Upper Saddle River, New Jersey, 2009.

Bennet, Jessica and Malcom Beith, Alternate Universe, Newsweek, July 30, 2007, pages 36-45.

Beugelsdijk, S., Hennart, J.-F., Slangen, A. & Smeets, R. 2010. Why and how FDI stocks are a biased measure of MNE affiliate activity. *Journal of International Business Studies*, 41(9):1444-1459.

Birkinshaw, J., Brannen, M.-Y., & Tung, R. L. 2011. From a distance and generalizable to up close and grounded: Reclaiming a place for qualitative methods in international business research. *Journal of International Business Studies*, 42(5): 573-581.

Blackstone, William T., The Search of an Environmental Ethic, in Tom Regan, Editor, Matters of Life and Death, Random House Inc., New York 1979.

Boatright, John, Ethics and the Conduct of Business, Fifth Edition, Pearson-Prentice Hall, Upper Saddle River, New Jersey 2007.

Bochoris Giorgos, European Model of Business Excellence & Framework for EKE (EFQM), EBEN Gr Model Workshop "Performance assessment & CSR", Athens 27th November 2007.

Boeh, K. S. & Beamish, P. W. 2012. Travel time and liability of distance in foreign direct investment: Location choice and entry mode. *Journal of International Business Studies*, 43(5): 525-535.

Brady, Diane, The Education of Jeff Immelt, BusinessWeek, April 29, 2002.

Bresman, H., Birkinshaw, J. & Nobel, R. 2010. Knowledge transfer in international acquisitions. *Journal of International Business Studies*, 41(1): 5-20.

Brock, R. H. 1978. *The Anti-trust Paradox: A Policy at War with Itself.* New York: Basic Books.

Brock, Robert H., The Anti-trust Paradox: A Policy at War with Itself, Basic Books, New York, 1978.

Brodbeck, F et al.2000. Cultural Variation of Leadership Prototypes Across 22 European Countries, Journal of Occupational and Organizational Psychology, March, 73 (2).1-29.

Brother's Keeper?, The Economist, April 20, 2002.

Budget for $17,000 in Athens, *Fortune, Volume 1, Number 4, May 1930, page 96.*

Byrne, J . (July 8,2002). Inside McKinsey, Bloomberg Businessweek. Available on line at
http://www.businessweek.com/magazine/content/02_27/b3790001.htm
Accessed 20/06/2011.

Byrne, John A., et al., How to Fix Corporate Governance, BusinessWeek, May 6, 2002, pages 43-50.

Byrne, John A., Inside McKinsey, BusinessWeek, July 8, 2002, pages 54-62.

Byrnes, Nanette and Mara Der Hovanesian, Earnings: A cleaner look, BusinessWeek, May 27, 2002, pages 32-35.

Byrnes, Nanette et al, The Good CEO, BusinessWeek, September 23, 2002, pages 44-54.

Byrnes, Nanette, et al., Accounting in crisis, BusinessWeek, January 28, 2002, pages 50-54.

Cantwell, J., Dunning, J. H. & Lundan, S. M. 2010. An evolutionary approach to understanding international business activity: The co-evolution of MNEs an d the institutional environment. *Journal of International Business Studies*, 41(4): 567-586.

Cappelli P., 1999. *The New Deal at Work: Managing the Market-Driven Workforce.* Boston, MA: Harvard Business School Press.

Cappelli P., The New Deal at Work: Managing the Market-Driven Workforce, Harvard Business School Press, Boston, MA 1999.

Carney, J. (March 2, 2011). Will Rajat Gupta destroy McKinsey
http://www.cnbc.com/id/41868799/Will_Rajat_Gupta_Destroy_McKinsey

Cavusgil, S. Tamer, Gary Knight and John R. Riesenberger, International Business: Strategy, Management and the New Realities, Pearson-Prentice Hall, Upper Saddle River, New Jersey 2008.

Chang, S.-J., Witteloostuijn, A. & Eden, L. 2010. From the Editors: Common method variance in international business research. *Journal of International Business Studies*, 41(1): 178-184.

Choi, Frederick D. S., Carol Ann Frost and Gary K. Meek, International Accounting, Third Edition, Prentice Hall, Upper Saddle River, New Jersey 1999.

Christmann, P. & Taylor, G. 2006. Firm self-regulation through international certifiable standards: determinants of symbolic versus substantive interpretation, *Journal of International Business Studies*, 37(6): 863-878.

Christmann, Petra and Glen Taylor, Firm serf-regulation through international certifiable standards: determinants of symbolic versus substansive interpretation, Journal of International Business Studies, Volume 37, Number 6, November 2006, σελίδες 863-878.

Chytiris Leonidas, Human Resources Management, Interbooks, Athens 2001.

Citizen first: Maps Obligations to Consumers, Ministry of Transport and Communication, Group of project management: Quality for citizens 1998.

Coggan, Philip, The tyranny of the benchmarks, Financial Times, June 8-9, 2002, page 18.

Cooper, D. 1971, *The Death of the Family*. London, UK: Allen Lane, The Penguin Press.

Cooper, David, The Death of the Family, Allen Lane, The Penguin Press, London, 1971.

Copeland, Michael V., Solar stocks for a rainy day, Fortune, European Edition, November 17, 2008 pages 43-46.

Corporate Social Responsibility:50+Good Practice, Greek Network for Corporate Social Responsibility, Athens 2005.

Coy, Peter, Housing Meltdown, BusinessWeek, February 11, 2008, σελίδες 42-46.

Coy, Peter, Why better numbers really matter, BusinessWeek, May 27, 2002, pages 34-35.

Cruver, B. (2002), Anatomy of greed: The unshredded truth from an Enron insider, Carroll and Graf.

Cuervo-Gazurra, A. 2006. Who cares about corruption? *Journal of International Business Studies*, 37(6): 807-822.

Cuervo-Gazurra, A. 2008. The effectiveness of laws against bribery abroad. *Journal of International Business Studies*, 39(4): 634-651.

Cuervo-Gazurra, Alvaro, Who cares about corruption? Journal of

International Business Studies, Volume 37, Number 6, November 2006, σελίδες 807-822.

Curry, Tilden J., Teaching Business Ethics: The Perspective of One Business Dean, Krishna S. Dhir, Editor, The Dean's Perspective, Decision Science Institute, Atlanta, Georgia 2008, pages 88-93.

Davidow, W. H. & Malone, S. M. 1993. *The Virtual Corporation: Restructuring and Revitalizing the Corporation for the 21st Century.* New York: Harper Business.

Davidow, William H. & Michael S. Malone The Virtual Corporation: Restructuring and Revitalizing the Corporation for the 21st Century, Harper Business, New York 1993.

Deal T and Kennedy, A 1982. Corporate cultures. Mass: Addison Wesley

DeGeorge, Richard T., Business Ethics, Sixth Edition, Pearson/Prentice Hall, Upper Saddle River, NJ 2006.

Demography and the West (Special Report), The Economist, August 24, 2002, pages 20-22.

Demosthenes, Demosthenes Speeches,Olynthiakoi B,editions Papyros, Athens

Derensky, H. 2008. *International Management: Managing Across Borders and Cultures*, Sixth Edition. Upper Saddle River, NJ: Pearson-Prentice Hall.

Derensky, Helen, International Management: Managing Across Borders and Cultures, Sixth Edition, Pearson-Prentice Hall, Upper Saddle River, New Jersey 2008.

Dervitsioti Kosta and Athanasiou Lagodimou, Business Competitiveness: Analysis-Development-Strategies, 2nd edition,Economic Library,Athens 2007.

Desjardins, Joseph R., Business Ethics and the Environment: Imagining a Sustainable Future, Pearson-Prentice Hall, Upper Saddle River, New Jersey 2007.

Devall, Bill, Simple in Means, Rich in Ends, Practicing Deep Ecology, Peregrine Smith Books, Salt Lake City UT 1988.

Dickey, Christopher, Fears in the 'Un-America', Newsweek, 11 February 2002, page 10.

Donaldson, T. 1966. Values in Tension: Ethics Away from Home. *Harvard Business Review.* September-October: 48-62.

Donaldson, Thomas, Values in Tension: Ethics Away from Home, Harvard Business Review, September-October 1996, pages 48-62.

Doukas Petros G., Corporate Governance, Capital markets, Stock exchange & Business Assessment, Institute of the Republic "Konstantinos Karamanlis, Studies of Political Economy & Diplomacy, I.Sideris, Athens 2002.

Drucker, Peter F., Management: Tasks, Responsibilities, Practices, Harper and Row, New York 1974.

Drucker, Peter, Survey of the near future: The next society, The Economist, November 3, 2001, pages 3-22.

Dunkelberg, John and Donald P. Robin, The Anatomy of Fraudulent Behavior, Business Horizons, November-December 1998, pages 77-82.

Early, P.C 2006. Leading cultural research in the future: A matter of paradigms and taste: Journal of International Business Studies, 37 (6) 922-931.

Eden, L. 2010. Letter from the Editor-in-Chief: Scientists behaving badly. *Journal of International Business Studies*, 41(4): 561-566.

Editorial, A Back-to-Basics Year, BusinessWeek, April 29, 2002.

Edmondson, Gail and Kate Carliste, Italy and the Eco-Mafia, BusinessWeek, January 27, 2003, pages 15-22.

Edwards, Mike, Lethal Legacy: Pollution in the Former U.S.S.R., National Geographic, August 1994.

Emmott, Bill, Our law, your law (μέρος της A Survey of America's world role), The Economist, June 29, 2002.

Enron Code of Ethics, Available on line at: http://bobsutton.typepad.com/files/enron-ethics.pdf Accessed 15 /06/2011.

Environmental enemy No. 1, The Economist, July 6th, 2002.

Faris, Stephan, The Other Side of Carbon Trading, Fortune Magazine, European Edition, September 3, 2007

Ferousis Dimitris S., Style and Ethics, Interbooks, Athens 1995.

Filos Giannis. Systems of Business Internal Audit, Editions IQ Group, Athens 2004.

Fischer, R.2008.Multilevel approaches in organizational settings: Opportunities, challenges and implications for cross cultural research, In F.J.R. van de Vijver, D.A. van Hemert & Y. Poortinga (Eds) Individuals and Cultures in Multi-level Analysis, pp. 173-196. Mahwah, NJ: Lawrence Erlbaum Associates.

Fisher, Colin and Alan Lovell, Business Ethics and Values, Finacial Time-Prentice Hall, Pearson Education Ltd, Harlow, England 2003.

Floridi, Luciano, *The fourth revolution: How the infosphere is reshaping human reality*. Oxford University. 2014.

Floridi, Luciano, The information society and its philosophy: Introduction to the special issue on "The philosophy of information, its nature, and future developments, *The information society*, Volume 25, 2009, pages 153–158.

Floridi, Luciano, Open problems in the philosophy of information, *Metaphilosophy,* Volume 35, Number 4, 2004, pages 554–582.

Foot, Margaret, and Caroline Hook, Introducing Human Resource Management, 4th Edition, FT Prentice Hall, London 2005.

Fotopoulos Christos and Athanasios Krystallis, The Greek consumer of Biological products: a national research of Marketing, Athens 2002.

Foust, Dean, The Best Performers of 2008 (The *BW* 50), *BusinessWeek*, April 7, 2008, pages 51-73.

Fowler, T. (October 20, 2002). The pride and the fall of Enron. Available on line at: http://www.chron.com/business/enron/article/Enron-s-corporate-tumble-was-a-long-time-coming-2083723.php

Fox, L. (2003), The rise and fall of Enron, NJ, John Wiley and Sons.

Furrer, Mariella and Gobris Saba, Keeping Alive, *Forbes Global*, 20 January 2003, pages 34-38.

Galbraith, John Kenneth, The New Industrial State, New American Library, New York 1967.

Garrett, Laurie, The Coming Plague, Penguin Books, London 1995.

Giannaras Christos, The decade as a challenge, A.A.Livani, Athens 1999

Gikas Socrates, Ancient Greeks Serious and Funny, Savalas, Athens 2002.

Gikas Socrates, New Philosophic Dictionary, Editions Savala, Athens 2002.

Giroux H.A. 2010 The Mouse that Roared: Disney and the End of Innocence by Henry A. Giroux and Grace Pollock Rowman & Littlefield Publishers Apr 16, 2010.

Goleman, D. 1995. *Emotional Intelligence: Why it can matter more than IQ*. New York: Batman Books.

Goleman, Daniel, Emotional Intelligence: Why it can matter more than IQ, Batman Books, New York 1995.

Goodman, Ted, Editor, The Forbes Book of Business Quotations, Konemann, Cologne, Germany 1999.

Goodpaster, K. E. and K. M. Sayre, Editors, Ethics and Problems of the 21st Century, University of Notre Dame Press, Notre Dame, IN 1979.

Greene, Robert, The 48 Laws of Power, Penguin Books, New York 2000.

Griffin, Ricky W. and Michael Pustay, International Business: A managerial Perspective, Fifth Edition, Pearson-Prentice Hall, Upper Saddle River, New Jersey 2007.

Grosvenor, Gilbert M., Will We Mend Our Earth? National Geographic, Volume 174, No. 6, December 1988.

Gunther, Marc, Doing well by clearing the air, Fortune, European Edition, November 17, 2008, pages 39-41.

Habib, Moshin and Leon Zurawicki, Corruption and Foreign Direct Investment, Journal of International Business Studies, Volume 33, No 2, Second Quarter 2002, pages 291-307.

Hadington Samuel, Comparison of Cultures and reformation of International Class, 3rd publication, Terzobooks, Athens 2001.

Hage, H. and Finsterbush, K.1987. Organizational Change as Development Strategy: Models and Tactics for Improving Third World Organizations, Lynne Rienner Publishers.

Hammer, Michael and James Champy, Reengineering the Corporation: A Manifesto for Business Revolution, Harper Business, New York 1993.

Hartman, Laura P., Perspectives in Business Ethics, Second Edition, McGraw-Hill Irwin, New York 2002.

Harvard Business Review on Corporate Governance, Harvard Business School Press, Boston, MA 2000.

Harvard Business Review on Corporate Responsibility, Harvard Business School Press, Boston, MA 2003.

Harzing, A.W 1999. Publish or perish. http://www.harzing.com/pop.htm

Hashmi, M. Anaam and Faramarz Damanpour, Cost of Corruption and Implications for MNCs: Special Focus on South Asia, The Journal of Current Research in Global Business, Fall 2002, pages 39-47.

Hawking, Stephen, The Universe in a Nutshell, Bantam Press, London, England 2001.

Helyar, J, Hymowitz, C and Srivastava, M. (May 17, 2011). Gupta secretly defied mcKInsey before SEC tip accusation, Available on line at: http://www.bloomberg.com/news/2011-05-17/gupta-secretly-defied-mckinsey-before-sec-s-tipster-accusation.html Accessed 20/06/2011.

Henry, David, Tom Lowry and Catherine Yang, AOL, you 've got misery, BusinessWeek, April 8, 2002.

Hickson, D.J.1974. The Culture-Free Context of Organization Structure: A Trinational Comparison, Sociology. 8 (1). 59-80.

Hill, A. (March 3, 2011). McKinsey faces risks as Gupta case unfolds.Financial Times. Available on line at: http://www.ft.com/intl/cms/s/0/68c2c834-45bf-11e0-acd8-00144feab49a.html#axzz1ZQyWrFua

Hill, C. E., Loch, K. D., Straub, D. W. and El-Sheshai, K, A.1998. Qualitative Assessment of Arab Culture and Information Technology Transfer, Journal of Global Information Management. 6(3).29-38.

Hofstede, G 1980. Culture`s consequences: International differences in work related values, Beverly Hills, CA: Sage

Hofstede, G 1991. Cultures and organizations: software of the mind. London: Mc Graw Hill.

Hofstede, G 2001. Culture`s consequences: Comparing values, behaviours, institutions and organizations across nations. Thousand Oaks, CA: Sage

Hofstede, G.1984. National cultures and corporate cultures. in Samovar L.A and Porter, R.E (Eds.), Communication Between Cultures. Belmont, CA: Wadsworth.

Hofstede, G.2006.What did GLOBE really measure? Researchers` minds vs respondents` minds.Journal of International Business Studies. 37(6).882-896.

Hofstede, Geert, National cultures in four dimensions, International Studies of Management and Organization, 1983, pages 46-74.

House, R.J, Hanges, P.J, Javidan, M., Dorfman, P.W and Gupta, V. 2004. Culture, leadership and organizations: The GLOBE study of 62 societies. Thousand Oaks, CA: Sage.

Hovanesian, Mara de, Christofer Palmeri, Nanette Byrnes, and Jessica Silver-Greenberg, Over the Limit, BusinessWeek, February 18, 2008, pages 34-37.

Ioannis Koukiadis, Labor Law: Individual Industrial Relations and the Law of Labor Flexibility, 3rd publication, Editions SAkoula, Athens 2005, page 563.

Issues 2002, special edition on Davos, Newsweek, December 2001-February 2002.

Jacoby, S. 1985. *Employing Bureaucracy: Managers, Unions, and the Transformation of Work in the American Industry, 1900-1945*. New York: Columbia University Press.

Jacoby, Sanford M. Employing Bureucracy: Managers, Unions, and the Transformation of Work in the American Industry, 1900-1945, Columbia University Press, New York 1985.

Javidan, M., House, R.J., Dorfman, P.W., Hanges, P.J., and Sully de Lugue, M., 2006.Conceptualizing and measuring cultures and their consequences: A comparative review of GLOBE`s and Hofstede`s approaches.Journal of International Business Studies. 37 (6). 897-914.

Kakabadse A. 1993. Success levers for Europe: the Cranfield Executive Competencies Survey. Journal of Management Development 13(1), 75-96.

Jeanjean, Thomas, Hervé Stolowy, Michael Erkens and Teri Lombardi Yohn, International evidence on the impact of adopting English as an external reporting language, *Journal of International Business Studies,* Volume 46, Issue 2 (February/ March 2015), pages 180-205.

Joshi, Amol M and Nandini Lahiri, Language friction and partner selection in cross-border R&D alliance formation, *Journal of International Business Studies,* Volume 46, Issue 2 (February/ March 2015), pages 123-152.

Karakatsanis Alexandros and Stavros Gardikas, Private Labor Law, 5th publication, Editions A.N Sakoula, Athens 1995.

Kennedy, Carol, Guide to the Management Gurus, Random House Business Books, London, England 1998.

King, Ralph, Forgiven, Business 2.0, November 2002, σελίδες 81-89.

Kirkpatrick, D. 2007. How Microsoft conquered China? Available on line at http://money.cnn.com/magazines/fortune/fortune_archive/2007/07/23/10 0134488/index.htm (accessed 12/01/2011)

Klein, N. 2007. *The Shock Doctrine: The Rise of Disaster Capitalism*. London, UK: Allen Lane-Penguin Books.

Klein, Naomi, The Shock Doctrine: The Rise of Disaster Capitalism, Allen Lane-Penguin Books, London 2007.

Kluckhohn, F. R. and Strodtbeck, F. L. 1961. Variations in value orientations. Evanston, Illinois: Row, Peterson.

Knorr A. and Arndt A. 2003. Why Wal-Mart fail in Germany?. Materialien des Wissenschaftsschwerpunktes "Globalisierung der Weltwirtschaft" Band 24 - Institut für Weltwirtschaft und Internationales Management. Universität Bremen.Deutschland.

Kochan T. and P. Cappelli, The Transformation of Industrial Relations and Personnel Function, in Paul Osterman's Editor, Internal Labor Market, MIT Press, Cambridge, MA 1984.

Kossek, Ellen Ernst και Richard N. Block, Managing Human Resources in the 21st Century: From Core Concepts to Strategic Choice, South-Western College Publishing, Cincinnati, Ohio 2000.

Kotler, Philip, Marketing Management: Analysis, Planning, Implementation and Control, Ninth International Edition, Prentice Hall International Inc., Upper Saddle River, New Jersey 1997.

Koulouri Vasili, Limit of arbitration in balancing accounts, Kathimerini,3rd March 2002.

Kovach, Kenneth, A. Sandra J. Conner, Tamar Livneh, Kevin M. Scallan and Roy S. Schwartz, Electronic Communication in the Workplace-Something's Got to Give, Business Horizons, July/August 2000, pages 59-64.

Kroeber, A.L. and Kluckhohn, C. 1952. Culture: A critical review of concepts and definitions. Harvard University Peabody Museum of American Archeology and Ethnology Papers 47.

Kwok, C. & Solomon, T. 2006. The MNC as an agent of change for host-country institutions. *Journal of International Business Studies*, 37(6): 767-785.

Kwok, Chuck FY and Solomon Todesse, The MNC as an agent of change for host-country institutions, Journal of International Business Studies, Volume 37, Number 6, November 2006: σελίδες 767-785.

Lavelle, Louis, The Best and Worst Boards, BusinessWeek, October 7, 2002, pages 58-64.

Leonard, K. D.1977. Reaching the Peasant Farmer: Organization Theory and Practice in Kenya. Chicago: The University of Chicago Press.

Lowrance, William W., Of Acceptable Risk, William Kaufmann, Inc., Los Altos, CA 1976.

Lubatkin, M., Ndiaye,M. and Vengroff, R.1997. The Nature of Managerial Work in Developing Countries: A Limited Test of the Universalist Hypothesis, Journal of International Business Studies, 28 (4):711-733.

Luigi, Ricci, *Machiavelli Niccolo: The Prince*, Institute of Medieval Studies, 1943, Toronto, Canada.

Luo, Y. 2006. Political behavior, social responsibility, and perceived corruption: a structuration perspective, *Journal of International Business Studies*, 37(6): 747-766.

Luo, Yadong, Political behavior, social responsibility, and perceived corruption: a structuration perspective, Journal of International Business Studies, Volume 37, Number 6, November 2006, σελίδες 747-766.

Lyons, Daniel, Full Disclosure, Forbes Global, April 2, 2002.

Maliaris Petros G.Introduction to Marketing,3rd publication, editions Stamouli Athens 2001.

Mandel, Michael, How real was the prosperity? Businessweek, February 4, 2008, pages 24-27.

Marie, Henrietta, Last Voyage of the Slave Ship, National Geographic, August 2002.

Marschall, S, Vaiman, V, Napier, N, Taylor, S, Haslberger, A and Andersen T, (2010), "The end of a "period": sustainability and the questioning attitude", *Academy of Management Learning and Education*, Vol.9, No.3, pp.477-487.

Maseland, R and Van Hoorn, A.2009. Explaining the negative correlation between values and practices: A note on the Hofstede GLOBE debate. Journal of International Business Studies. 40 (3).527-532.

Matthews, Samuel W., Under the Sun: Is Our World Warming? National Geographic, October 1990.

McGregor, D. 1960. *The Human Side of Enterprise*. New York: McGraw-Hill Books Company, Inc.

McGregor, Douglas, The Human Side of Enterprise, McGraw-Hill Books Company, Inc, New York 1960.

McGregor, Jena, Consumer vigilantes, BusinessWeek, March 3, 2008, pages 38-42.

McGregor, Jena, The 2008 Winners, BusinessWeek, March 3, 2008, pages 47-52.

McIntosh, Malcom, Ruth Thomas, Deborah Leipziger and Gill Coleman, Living Corporate Citizenship: Strategic Routes to Socially Responsible Business, FT Prentice Hall, London 2003.

McLuhan, M. M. 1967. *La Galaxie Gutenberg Face à l'Ere Electronique.* Paris, France : Mame.

McLuhan, Marshall M., La Galaxie Gutenberg Face à l'Ere Electronique, Mame, Paris, France, 2η γαλλική έκδοση, 1967.

McNamee, Mike, Amy Borus and Christopher Palmeri, Out of Control at Andersen, BusinessWeek, April 8, 2002.

McSweeney, B.2002.Hofstede`s model of national cultural differences and their consequences: A triumph of faith; a failure of analysis, Human Relations, 55 (1). 89-118.

Meyer, Harvey, The Greening of Corporate America, Journal of Business Strategy, January-February 2000, pages 38-43.

Mintzberg, H.1973. Managerial Work. NY: Harper and Row.

Mitchell, John G., Our Polluted Runoff, National Geographic, February 1996,

Morais, Richard C., The stakes get higher, Forbes Global, April 29, 2002.

Morris, Betsy, The Pepsi challenge: Can this snack and soda giant go healthy?, Fortune, March 3, 2008, pages 42-50.

Morris, Tom, If Aristotle Ran General Motors: The New Soul of Business, Henry Holt and Company, New York 1997.

Moshin, H. & Zurawicki, L. 2002. Corruption and Foreign Direct Investment, *Journal of International Business Studies*, 33(2): 291-307.

Murray, Sarah, Corporate Social Responsibility: Now is the time to clarify the true meaning, Financial Times, January 21, 2002, Supplement on business education, page 10.

Murray, Sarah, The fight against fakes is far from over, Financial Times, 6-7 April 2002, page 5.

Myers, A., Kakabadse, A., McMahon, T. and Spony, G. 1995. Top Management Styles in Europe: Implications for Business and Cross-national Teams, European Business Journal, 7(1):17-28.

Nachum, L. & Song, S. 2011. The MNE as a portfolio: Interdependencies in MNE growth trajectory. *Journal of International Business Studies*, 42(3): 381-405.

Naughton, Keith, Small. It's the new Big, Newsweek, February 25, 2008, pages 34-37.

Newman, K. and Nollen, S.1996. Culture and Congruence: The Fit Between Management Practices and National Culture, Journal of International Business Studies,27(4): 753-779.

Novak, M. (1996) Business as a Calling: Work and the Examined Life. New York: The Free

Nuclear dawn, The Economist Technology Quarterly, September 8, 2007, pages 20-22.

Nussbaum, Bruce, Can you trust anybody anymore, BusinessWeek, January 28, 2002, pages 39-40.

Ó Tuathail Gearoid, Simon Dalby and Paul Routledge, Editors, *The Geopolitics Reader,* Second Edition, Routledge, London and New York 2006.

O' Blenes, Carole, Harassment grows more complex, Management Review, June 1999, pages 49-51.

Official Gazette of the E.C. 2-12-2000, Directive 2000/78/E.C. of the Council Dated:27-11-2000.

Official Gazette of the Greek republic,1st volume,No 191,11th September 2006, L.3488.

Orwell, G. 2008 (initially published in 1949). *1984.* London, UK: Penguin Books.

Ory, Michael, A Food Fight Over Calorie Counts, BusinessWeek, February 11, 2008, page 36.

Ouchi, W.G 1981.Theory Z: How American business can meet the Japanese challenge. Reading Mass: Addison Wesley

Papanoutsos Evangelos P. Ethics, Icarus, Athens 1949.

Papanoutsos Evangelos P. The Law of Fist, Dodoni Athens 1975.

Park, Hoon, unpublished presentation on the Determinants of Corruption: A Cross-national Analysis, Annual Conference of the Association for Global Business, Las Vegas, Nevada, November 22, 2002.

Pascale, R.T and Athos, A 1981. The art of Japanese management. NY: Simon Schuster.

Pasternack, B. A. & Viscio, A.J. 1998. *The Centerless Corporation: A New Model for Transforming your Organization for Growth and Prosperity.* New York: Simon and Schuster.

Pasternack, Bruce A., and Albert J. Viscio, The Centerless Corporation: A New Model for Transforming your Organization for Growth and Prosperity, Simon and Schuster, New York, 1998.

Pelled, L. and Xin,K.1997. Work Values and their Human Resource Management Implications: A Theoretical Comparison of China, Mexico, and the United States, Journal of Applied Management Studies, 6 (2): 185-198.

Pericles Epitaph, Greek parliament, 1998, pages 32-33.

Perrault, Jr., William D. and E. Jerome McCarthy, Basic Marketing: A Global Mnagerial Approach, Twelfth International Edition, Irwin-

McGraw-Hill, Boston, 1996.

Peters, T and Waterman, R. 1982. In search of excellence: Lessons from Americas best run companies: NY: Harper Row

Peterson, M. F., Arregle, J.-L. & Martin, X. 2012. Multilevel models in international business research. *Journal of International Business Studies*, 43(5): 451-457.

Plakoyiannaki, Emmanuella, Kalliopi Mathioudaki, Pavlos Dimitratos, Yorgos Zotos, Images of Women In Online Advertisements of Global Products: Does Sexism Exist? Journal of Business Ethics, Volume 83, Number 1, Spring 2008.

Promoting a European framework for Corporate Social Responsibility, (Green paper, COM(2001) 416 final, Commission of the European Communities 2000.

Rand, A. 1964. *The Virtue of Selfishness*. New York: New American Library.

Rand, Ayn, The Virtue of Selfishness, New American Library, New York 1964.

Redman, Tom and Andrian Wilkinson, *Contemporary Human Resource Management*, Seventh Edition, Pearson Education 2006.

Reeb, D., Sakakibara, M. & Mahmood, I. P. 2012. From the Editors: Endogeneity in international business research. *Journal of International Business Studies*, 43(3): 211-218.

Reich, R. B. 2007. *Supercapitalism: The Transformation of Business, Democracy and Everyday Life.* New York: Random House.

Reich, Robert B., *Supercapitalism: The Transformation of Business, Democracy and Everyday Life*, Random House, New York 2007.

Reischhl, Thomas C., Ethics and Customer Service, National Underwriter, Cincinnatti, Ohio 1999.

Richardson, John E. Editor, Business Ethics 01/02, Thirteenth Edition, Annual Editions McGraw-Hill/Dushkin, Guilford, Connecticut 2001.

Rodriguez, P., Siegel, D. S., Hillman, A. & Eden, L. 2006. Three levels of the multinational enterprise: politics, corruption, and corporate social responsibility. *Journal of International Business Studies*, (43)6: 733-746.

Rodriguez, Peter, Donald S. Siegel, Amy Hillman, and Lorraine Eden, Three levels of the multinational enterprise: politics, corruption, and corporate social responsibility, Journal of International Business Studies, Volume 37, Number 6, November 2006, σελίδες 733-746.

Rossant, John A Fragile World, *BusinessWeek*, February 11, 2002, page 24.

Rossant, John Fortress Switzerland, *BusinessWeek*, June 4, 2001, pages 22-23.

Rossant, John, Jack Ewing and Brian Bremner, The Corporate Cleanup Goes Global, Business Week, May 6, 2002, pages 52-53.

Rugman, A. M. & Verbeke, A. 2004. A perspective of regional and global strategies of multinational enterprises. *Journal of International Business Studies*, 35(1): 3-18.

Salk, J. E. and Brannen,M.Y.2000. National Culture, Networks, and Individual Influence in a Multinational Management Team, Academy of Management Journal, 43, (2):191-202.

Salter, James, It's not the old Point, *Life Magazine*, May 1980, pages 70-79.

Santangelo, G. D. & Meyer, K. E. 2011. Increases and decreases of MNE commitment in emerging economies. *Journal of International Business Studies*, 42(7): 894-909.

Schein, E.H.1992. Organizational Culture and Leadership: A Dynamic View, 2nd edition, CA: Jossey-Bass, San Francisco.

Scherer, Donald and Thomas Attig, Editors, *Ethics and the Environment*, Prentice Hall, Englewood Cliffs, NJ 1983.

Schwab, Klaus, Off the Couch, Special Edition: Issues 2008, *Newsweek*, page 21.

SEV, volume 620, May 2005.

Selmier II, W., Travis Aloysius Newenham-Kahindi and Chang Hoon Oh, Understanding the words of relationships: Language as an essential tool to manage CSR in communities of place, *Journal of International Business Studies,* Volume 46, Issue 2 (February/ March 2015), pages 153-179.

Skelly, J. 1995. The Caux Round Table: Principles for Business, The Rise of International Ethics. *Business Ethics*, March-April: 2-5(supplement).

Skelly, Joe, The Caux Round Table: Principles for Business, The Rise of International Ethics, *Business Ethics*, March-April 1995, pages 2-5-supplement.

Sloan, Allan και Michael Isikoff, The Enron Effect, *Newsweek*, 28 January 2002, page 40.

Smith Craig, N. and Quirk, M. (2004), "From Grace to Disgrace: The rise and fall of Arthur Andersen", *Journal of Business Ethics Education*, Vol.1, No.1, pp.91-130.

Squires, S, Smith, C, McDougall, L and Yeack, W. (2003), Inside Arthur Andersen: Shifting values, unexpected consequences, NJ, FT Press.

Stanwick, Peter A. and Sarah D. Stanwick, *Understanding Business Ethics*, Pearson-Prentice Hall, Upper Saddle River, New Jersey 2009.

Stephan U. and Uhlaner M. 2010. Performance based vs socially responsible culture: A cross national study of descriptive norms and entrepreneurship. Journal of International Business Studies. 41 (8), pp.1347-1364.

Stewart, Creg L. and Kenneth G. Brown, *Human Resource Management: Linking Strategy to Practice*, John Wiley and Sons, Inc., Hoboken, NJ 2009.

Sustaining the poor's development, *The Economist*, August 31st, 2002, page 11.

Swartz M., Watkins S., Power failure: The inside story of the collapse of Enron, Crown Business, 2004.

Swartz, M., Watkins, S., Power failure: The inside story of the collapse of Enron, Crown Business, 2004.

Swindler, A. 1986. Culture in action: Symbols and strategies. American Sociological Review, 51 (2). 273-286

Tale of two bellies, *The Economist*, August 24, 2002, page 11.

Tayeb, M. 1996. The Management of a Multicultural Workforce. Chichester: Wiley & Sons.

Tayeb, M.1994. Organizations and National Culture: Methodology Considered, Organization Studies: Special Issue on Cross-National Organization Culture, 15(3): 429-446.

Thanopoulos Ioannis, Business in our International Village, Interbooks, Athens 2002.

Thanopoulos Ioannis, International Business:Environment , Structure and Challenges Interbooks, Athens 2006.

Thanopoulos, John and Ivan R. Vernon," International Business Education in the AACSB Schools," *Journal of International Business Studies*, Volume 18, Number 1 (1987), pages 91-98.

Thanopoulos, John and with Charles Little, "The Brave New Global Enterprise," *Review of Business*, Volume 20 (Number 2) Winter 1998, page 3.

Thanopoulos, John and with L. L. Schkade, "Towards Global Entrepreneurialism," *North Central Business Journal*, Volume I, Issue 7, Summer/Fall 2000, pages 46-7.

Thanopoulos, John, "How to Add Philosophy Dimensions in Your Basic International Business Course," *Journal of Teaching in International Business*, Volume 21 (Issue 3), July-September 2010, pages 189-199.

Thanopoulos, John, *Business Ethics in the Era of Corporate Governance*, Second edition, Interbooks, Athens, Greece 2009.

Thanopoulos, John, *Global Business: Environment, Structure and Challenges*, Athens, Greece, Interbooks 2007.

Thanopoulos, John, *The Global Manager: Self actualization*

Perspectives, coauthored with 185 of his Fall 2009 students, first electronic edition (cd-rom), Interbooks, Athens 2010.

The 70s: The Decade in Pictures, *Life Magazine*, Special issue, December 1979.

The short arm of the law, *The Economist*, March 2, 2002, page 67.

The World in 2012, *Newsweek*, September 16, 2002.

The worm never dies, *The Economist*, March 2, 2002, page 11.

Theil, Stefan and Cristopher Dickey. Europe's Dirty Secrets, *Newsweek*, April 29, 2002, pages 14-19.

Thiroux, Jacques, *Ethics: Theory and Practice*, 6th Edition, Prentice Hall, Upper Saddle River, New Jersey, 1998.

Torrington, Derek, Laura Hall and Stephen Taylor, *Human Resource Management*, Sixth Edition, FT Prentice Hall, London 2005.

Tree, Isabella, Living Goddess of Nepal, *National Geographic*, June 2015, pages 78-97.

Trevino, Linda K. and Katherine A. Nelson, *Managing Business Ethics: Straight Talk About How To Do It Right*, Second Edition, John Wiley and Sons, New York 1999.

Trompenaars, F. 1993. Riding the Waves of Culture: Understanding Cultural Diversity in Business. London: Economist Books.

Tugenhat, Christopher, *The Multinationals,* Eyre & Spottiswoode, London 1971.

Tumulty, Karen, The making of a come-back, *Time Magazine*, November 25, 2002, pages 48-49.

Tung, R.L.2008. The cross cultural research imperative: The need to balance cross national and intra national diversity. Journal of International Business Studies. 39(1).41-46

Turbine time, *The Economist*, July 19, 2008, pages 45-46.

Tylor,E. 1871. Primitive Culture. New York: J.P. Putnam's Sons. 16.

Tzamalikos Panagiotis, philosophic Aspects of Technology Thessaloniki 1997.

Used Oil Pollution Outweighs Tanker Spills, Earth Almanac, *National Geographic*, March 1991.

Velasquez, Manuel G., *Business Ethics: Concepts and Cases*, Fourth Edition, Prentice Hall, Upper Saddle River, New Jersey, 1998.

Vencat, Emily Flynn and Ginanne Brownell, A life Behind Close Doors, Special Issue on Issues 2008, *Newsweek*, Executive life, pages 6-10.

Vengroff, R.1988. Rural Development, policy Reforms and the Assessment of Management Training Needs in Africa: A Comparative Perspective. Paper prepared for Delivery at the Annual Meeting of the African Studies Association, Chicago, October 27-30.

Waitley, Dennis, *Empires of Mind: Lessons to Lead and Succed in a*

Knowledge-based World, William Morrow and Company, New York 1995.

Ways, Max, Business faces growing pressures to behave better, *Fortune*, May 1974, pages 193-195, 314, 316, 319, 320.

Weber, Joseph, et al., Can Andersen survive, *BusinessWeek*, January 28, 2002, pages 46-47.

Weintraub, Ariene, Just Say No To Drug Reps, *Businessweek*, February 4, 2008 page 69.

Weiss, Joseph W., *Business Ethics: A Stakeholder and Issues Management Approach*, 3rd Edition, Thomson-South-Western, Mason, Ohio 2003.

Weitzel, U. & Berns, S. 2006. Cross-border takeovers, corruption, and related aspects of government. *Journal of International Business Studies*, (37)6: 786-806.

Weitzel, Utz and Sjors Berns, Cross-border takeovers, corruption, and related aspects of government, *Journal of International Business Studies*, Volume 37, Number 6, November 2006, pages 786-806.

Westney, D. E. & Maanen, J. 2011. The causal ethnography of the executive suite. *Journal of International Business Studies*, 42(5): 602-607.

What Is True? *Forbes-ASAP*, 2 October 2000.

Winocur, Mark, *Einstein, A Portrait*, Pomegranate Artbooks, Corte-Madera, CA.

Wolfe, Alan, It's all our fault, *Newsweek*, December 2001-February 2002, special issue on "Issues 2002", page 48.

Woody, Todd, Trying to catch the wind, *Fortune*, European Edition, November 17, 2008 pages 48-49.

WorldCom: Another cowboy bites the dust, *The Economist*, June 29, 2002.

Xenophon, Economic-Resources, editions Cactus,127,Athens, March 1993.

Yang, Jia Lynn Lessons in Leadership: The Three-Minute Manager, *Fortune*, December 24, 2007, page 64.

Zakaria, Fareed, A plan for global security, *Newsweek*, December 2001-February 2002, special issue on "Issues 2002", pages 16-17.

Zellner, Wendy and Stephanie Forest Anderson, A Hero-and a smoking-gun letter, *BusinessWeek*, January 28, 2002, pages 42-43.

Zikmund, William G. and Michael D' Amico, *Marketing,* 6th Edition, South-Western College Publishing, Cincinnati, Ohio, 1999.

"Some of the business ethics issues raised in this book"[219]

Introduction: Dear co-citizen of the planet Earth

... one may deduce that human nature with tendencies of deviance is egoistical, narcissistic, hedonistic, aplestos, greedy, self-serving always preferring to take the easy path instead of the virtuous, honest, hard-working and painful path to achievement. This negatively portrayed deviant human nature is the complete opposite of ethos and ethical behavior which are only cultivated by positive characteristics of human nature such as altruistic, philanthropic, epicuric and assistive to avail good utility to our fellow humans. (11)

Reflecting on the speculation "what is legal is also ethical" a critical thinker may deduce that the reduction of ethics down to bare legality provides only the minimum of morality.(12)

Sound and constantly upgraded specialization is a key factor to ethical management. (13)

Does "business" and "ethics" in the same sentence sound as oxymoron? (15)

The business organization wherever located and regardless of size or industry, has now become a crucial part of society and must reflect the philosophy and ethics of the people. (16)

CHAPTER 1: FROM PHILOSOPHY TO ETHICS
What is ethics? (25)

---

[219] The issues presented here are direct quotes from the book and, among others, they have been used for active learning and as question platforms for university-level undergraduate students since 2003. The students knowing that a "reward" is attached to the best answers they tended to read in advance the assigned material and go beyond it. The class size was 20-50 members, usually assigned as 5-member teams, although great results were obvious in classes ranging from 120-250 students. For more information on active learning please see subnote #14.

We are rewarded to follow instructions and obey rules. (26)

… the rules of conduct we have, just like a set of consciousness codes, are written in our hearts. (Apostle Paul, 27)

The best chance you have of making a big success in this world is to decide from square one that you are going to do it ethically. (Alan Greenspan, 28)

What is philosophy, what is truth? (28)

The speed of the message is the message. (30)

… the way we manipulate other people is primarily manipulating the truth, by bluffing, by a little deception, by lying." (Tom Morris, 31)

Technology creates barriers to our sense of truth. (32)

Ethics is the branch of philosophy dealing with values that are related to human behavior with regard to the appropriateness or inappropriateness of acts, their goodness or not, their motives or their purpose. (34)

… the texture of our universe is one where there is no question at all but that good, laughter and justice will prevail. (Archbishop Desmond Tutu, 36)

… justified is the man who tries, who exploits all the possibilities, free will and logic offer to him and from this process gains the most. (Archimandrite Konstantinos Papanikolaou, 39)

… it is impossible to live a pleasant life without living wisely and well and justly and it is impossible to live wisely and well and justly without living a pleasant life. (Epikouros, 40)

The duty of an individual is to enlighten and offer his ideas to the world. (Perelman, 41)

"There is no patent." Jonas Salk, inventor, vaccine for polio, 41)

"Know Yourself." (42)

… an action is ethical if produces the greatest good for most people. (42)

… do to others what they will want to do to you … (43)

... the era of societal globalization, international business and corporate governance has already imposed norms, situations and behavior that could not be predicted from the previous philosophers. (44)

What happens when the government allows obvious cases of bribing, or legal violations? (45)

"Pacta sunt servanda," agreements must be kept. (46)

There exists no crime and (therefore) no punishment without a pre-existing penal law. But who is establishing that law? Who is empowering this authority? (46)

... (the) conflict between business interests and ethics ... is entangled with a variety of mixed motives. (Stark, 49)

... females are more concerned with business ethics than males and college students in general show an increased interest, awareness and concern about business ethics. 50)

... people possessing the technology can set the new rules. (52)

... science becomes the servant of the powerful. (Henderson, 53)

Business faces growing pressures to behave better! (Max Ways, 54)

Truth is relative and expanding; it lives always in the present, achieving new expression in each generation of men. (Urantia, 56)

CHAPTER 2: THE SOCIETY OF THE 21ST CENTURY

"Freedom illuminates the world!" (Statue of Liberty, 59)

Large international corporations have turnover well above the GDP of most individual states or individual countries. (60)

Social transformation from the human in a group to the society of people. (Marshall M. McLuhan, 61)

Within their area people have developed their own lifestyles and behavior and their philosophical underpinnings and morality. (62)

Opening up national borders is very challenging especially during an economic crisis. (62)

People seeking identity and rediscovering their nationality, need enemies. (Huntington, 62)

Do we any longer need military enforcement mechanisms where the lack of barriers and globalization specify new types of business attack and enforcement? (65)

Today's revolutionaries have a limited understanding of the world. (65)

Beyond cultural and economic conflicts that require maintenance of military systems and development of transnational treaties and accords, there are other reasons, perhaps more tangible and largely associated with the overall evolution of a republic, highlighting the contrasts between countries and the distance between the people who "have" and the people who "have not". (67)

Consider economic reasons for population migration. (69)

Only in the last 100 years people were able to record reliably comparative statistics. (69)

Countries that were considered "developing", forty years ago, will far surpass the GDP of present 'developed' countries. (70)

… hyper-capitalism is determined by the continuous accumulation of the planet's wealth in fewer and fewer super-capitalists … (71)

The global institutions like GATT and then WTO, contribute to further reduce older trade barriers. The ground is therefore fertile to begin intergovernmental agreements of various types. (73)

… changes we observe in our environment depend on the level of economic development, which in turn depends on the progress of technology and thereby influence the philosophical and ethical mutations. (74)

… "new conditions" of modern life create different philosophical and ethical realities from those people who were accustomed to experiencing during the pre-technological era. (75)

Discuss effects of knowledge and technology in today's global society. (78)

Compare changes of philosophical and ethical thinking in the developed worlds during the last 50 years. (78)

CHAPTER 3: THE ERA OF THE GLOBAL CORPORATION

Practical experience has shown the industry-wide and the culture-specific difficulties in applying universally acceptable accounting standards. (83)

We should be particularly careful of systemic accounting solutions which were once acceptable and allowed but should be re-examined today. (84)

Governments cannot do everything. It is time for large corporations to enter the game. Corporate managers can help develop a methodology conducive to the development of the world but at the same time to achieve corporate objectives. (Schwab, 85)

Prerequisite of doing business is the existence of employee and customer-oriented administration, sensitive to social causes and the code of corporate governance. (86)

The basic generator of 21st century social change is the person-driven social systems of philosophy, ethics, regulations, laws and justice. (87)

The global corporation is now responsible for social change, production, research, development, education, and even happiness of employees. (90)

The largest 500 corporations, employing less than the 1/100 of the planet's population, produce more than 40% of the equivalent of the global GDP. (91)

"Living and working together for the common good." (Kyosei, 92)

"All people, regardless of race, religion or culture, harmoniously living and working together into the future." (Canon, 92)

"Most admired" or "the best company to work for" company: Think of the power of the media and their capacity to impose favorable images to the everyday citizen … (93)

We must "take care" of our global managers. As individuals they have few support mechanisms. They must have self-control. They think alone. They evolve by themselves. They are influenced by the mass media. Moreover, given their rapid professional growth, they do not have the time to develop the survival virtues of the old aristocracy. (94)

CHAPTER 4: THE MARKET AND THE CUSTOMER

Before 1960, even in more developed countries there were few laws that actually protected the consumer. (97)

Either, the customer will buy the product at the price and conditions offered by the monopoly, or will not enjoy it at all. (99)

The large global corporations are in a position to force local manufacturers to produce a better and a cheaper product. In contrast, the localized smaller enterprise is less effective. If a small business does not play by the rules of the producers it may be expelled from the market. (102)

The consumer should be able to evaluate the risk-cost basis. In other words, decide to reduce the risk by assuming a greater financial burden. (102)

The corporation, bringing a product to the market delivers an indirect contractual obligation to comply with the all promises made. (103)

Advertising creates a quasi-monopoly. Habitual behavior works as a second nature *forcing* buying decisions. (104)

The purpose of advertising is to manage and shape the consumer, which probably leads to restriction of choice and free will. (Galbraith, 105)

Has advertisement a potential of not being ethical by affecting the consumer buying behavior? (106)

In the post-war era, a revolution in retail occurs … purchasing products and services come with luxury establishments which offer, besides satisfaction with the product itself, a total experience where the consumer is experiencing this environment to the point it becomes a habit the frequent visit to it. (107)

Consider the reason for the existence of companies producing cigarettes or alcoholic beverages or companies that operate gambling centers? Is there an ethos to such companies, why, why not? (108)

The requirement for a "total" product to offer guarantees, true standards, sound advertising, contractual obligations, freedom of choice, (and so on) is motivated by our entrepreneurial era and modern social imperatives. (111)

Particularly in wealthy countries, and given an inclination to leisure, media proliferation and inability to focus on philosophical positions creates an artificial sense of self-indulgence for virtually nonexistent over-consumption needs. (111)

CHAPTER 5: THE CENTER OF OUR ATTENTION: THE EMPLOYEES!

Inspired management of human resources goes beyond the moral rights or legal obligations: It's a business necessity to attract talent and achieve corporate objectives. (115)

The after the industrial revolution era gave a new social status to the underprivileged, promoted education, changed the role that women had in the work force, established standards of life quality, allowed the worker "to reach his full potential." (116)

With respect to social ethics all people are acceptable in the workplace and are legally protected regardless of religious belief, sexual orientation, ethnic roots, race or color. (117)

Workers 'choose' their companies as the companies choose their employees so that there is harmony with the philosophy and culture of cooperation, expectations, visions and requirements. (119)

A global labor market will not make every individual in the world better off: there will be losers as well as winners. (Matthew Bishop, 120)

The 500 largest companies in the world are employing less than 1% of the world's population, indicative that they actively seek talented individuals to generate, in average, almost half a million US$ revenue per person employed. (122)

We are witnesses of a balance of rights and responsibilities of both employee and employer, from the convergence of principles and is related to the competitive environment, socioeconomic conditions, technological realities and legal requirements. (127)

CHAPTER 6: THE ENVIRONMENT, OUR HOME

People everywhere feel offense because of the environmental pollution. Subconsciously they feel we passed limits we shouldn't have. They want to clean the world, make it better and become the earth guardians for future generations. (Speth, 129)

The challenge is to ...start rebuilding a world which will be in an ecological and human balance. (Wiesner, 129)

Man's intervention to his environment is variable and it doesn't only concern its pollution. This is a question of philosophy and ethics at the personal, business and state levels. (131)

The existence of international conditions of environmental protection and international law, obligates single regulations to most countries, although strong countries, such as the USA or China, follow with their own will the commands of international community. (137)

Observe that the "platform" of ecological ethics should include items like:
Prosperity and evolution of "human" and "non-human" life on Earth have value themselves and
that types of life variety contributes to the real value. (138)

It is doubtful if logic of an ecological conscience can flow evenly in all manifestations of the modern business economy. (139)

Might our globalized society that offers more benefits to more people than ever, lead to a reality of respect not only towards every human or non-human species but to re-evaluation of every act, every omission and every process? (140)

CHAPTER 7: FINANCE ISSUES AND THE CODE OF CORPORATE GOVERNANCE

Historically, the owners of the land and the capital were always self-serving! They understood human suffering and sacrifice and they capitalized on it: through armed forces, understanding of human submission, discipline, religion, law and education, which were the means of their power. They created their own wealth and imposed ethical behaviors to the masses. (143)

Today there exists sometimes latitude of ethical behavior from the part of the owners of the capital. (143)

In most parts of our planet we still experience lots of the pre-industrial era practices with respect to the financial yield. So, where is the light for capital owners' ethical behavior? (143)

Clearly in the 21st century the common man has gained a lot. Nevertheless, the commanders of wealth and of capital, as well as their immediate subordinates, venture their daily lives in two opposing directions: Some of them still live away from self-actualization mode, "employee happiness" and existentialist dimensions in secluded palaces, private jets, mega-yachts and superficial self-serving behaviors whereas the rest seems they understand that simplicity has to offer more than status quo ... (144)

Are we witnessing a new era of social and business ethics that focuses on the individual citizen? (144)

You are advised to note that changes of the existing enterprise resource planning systems may not be an easy task and often this has the potential of unethical repercussions, even of illegal ones, especially when confronted with cross-border transactions of financial interest. (145)

Corporate governance and its principles is something like the corporate "constitution" defining the responsibilities and relationships of all company stakeholders. (146)

The shareholders are the major influencers of changes that will affect the economic future of the company with grave ethical implications and ability to effect the new corporate order. (146)

A whole life time is required to build a good corporate reputation and only a short time to destroy it. (Neubauer, 148)

Without effective corporate governance business efforts will yield lower results than the original business plan sought. (149)

It could be said that the lack of effective corporate governance is unethical because it wastes social resources. (149)

Un-meritocracy in corporate governance is, in principle unethical. (149)

There is no existence of corporate governance without control mechanisms. (151)

To be somebody important, one must have virtues. To act someone correctly in politics and by extension in business, one must be of great morals. (Aristotle, 158)

While preparing a code of corporate governance avoid forced movements. Collect the necessary information from all stakeholders. Define the area of ethics concerned and study it. Find who and what it concerns.(159)

As a minimum the code of corporate governance should include the organizational positions towards its customers, employees, owners, supplier, competitors and the social environment. (162)

Epilogue: Living Together

Business itself has evolved so fast, that its philosophy as well as its processes of operating, auditing and total behavior are not as yet firmly grounded, in order to guarantee that its mechanism will not dictatorially rule the planet but will specify principles of spiritual evolution and emotional balance in a peaceful world. (165)

Arrogant, selfish and mostly materialistic demands or social resources' blatant waste should not be allowed. (166)

The burden for future social enhancement falls to the wise leaders of modern business, to their mentality, their education, the evaluation of their projects, their choices. (167)

Made in the USA
San Bernardino, CA
02 February 2017